P9-CET-760

SAINT PATRICK

ST. IGNATIUS CHURCH
Cascieri, Boston, sculptor

BOSTON COLLEGE
Bernardine Truden, donor.

PHOTO BY THE AUTHOR.

The Legacy of SAINT PATRICK

As found in his own writings

"So that after my death I may leave a legacy to my brethren and to my sons whom I baptized in the Lord."

Confession 14.

MARTIN P. HARNEY, S.J.

St. Paul Editions

Imprimi Potest:
REV. WILLIAM G. GUINDON, S.J.
Provincial, New England Province.

Nihil Obstat:
REV. JAMES A. O'DONOHOE, J.C.D.
Diocesan Censor

Imprimatur:
✠RICHARD CARDINAL CUSHING.

Library of Congress Catalog Card Number:
76–183441

Printed by the Daughters of St. Paul
50 St. Paul's Ave., Jamaica Plain, Boston, Ma. 02130

The Daughters of St. Paul are an international congregation of religious women serving the Church with the communications media.

TABLE OF CONTENTS

The Arms of Cardinal Conway.

To

His Eminence

WILLIAM CARDINAL CONWAY, D.D., D.C.L.

Archbishop of Armagh

Primate of All Ireland

Successor of St. Patrick

FOREWORD

The legacy of St. Patrick, which he would bequeath to his brethren and their descendants, was his own holy idealism. It can be found in his two writings, the *Confession of St. Patrick* and the *Letter to the Soldiers of Coroticus.* The saint puts it clearly: "Wherefore, I cannot keep silence—nor would it be fitting—considering such great benefits and such great graces as the Lord has vouchsafed to bestow on me in the land of my captivity; for this is the return we make, that after our chastening, or after our recognition of God, we should exalt and proclaim His wondrous ways before every nation which is under the whole heaven." (*Confession,* 3.) "Yet, although I am faulty in many things, I wish my brethren and kinsfolk to know what manner of man I am, so that they may be able to understand the desire of my soul." (*Confession,* 6.) "And so in the measure of our faith in the Trinity it is fitting for me to explain and without censure of rashness to make known the gift of God and the everlasting hope. Moreover it is fitting that I spread everywhere the name of God without fear, confidently: so that after my death I may leave a legacy to my brethren and my sons whom I have baptized in the Lord—so many thousands of men." (*Confession*, 14.)

Both documents, the *Confession* and the *Letter*, are accepted as authentic by all modern Patrician scholars. Both are brief works; printed together, they hardly fill thirty pages of a pamphlet. Yet they are supremely important, because they offer a clear and complete presentation of the spirituality of Ireland's apostle. A thoughtful perusal of the *Confession* and of the *Letter* will reward the reader with a true and an intimate knowledge of St. Patrick. Then will stand in the reader's vision the *real* St. Patrick.

How few know him! The St. Patrick of popular imagination is a semi-mythical character, a combination of medieval legendry and modern commercialism. Everywhere and always the Irish people have been unswerving in their devotion to their father-in-God; but their conception of him for the most part has been cloudy and vague. The reason is that they have not known him in his writings, except for a few quotations found in a book or heard in a sermon. To help for a truer knowledge of Ireland's apostle an English version of the complete texts of the *Confession* and the *Letter* has been made the heart of this book. An attentive reading of both these authentic writings of St. Patrick will reveal why Professor MacNeill could write: "No one has ever left so strong and permanent impression of his personality on a people, with the single and eminent exception of Moses." Reading St. Patrick's two writings will be of profit also for his numerous non-Irish admirers; it will widen their knowledge of him and it will afford them rich inspirations. St. Patrick's idealism bears an appeal for men of good will everywhere.

If a personal note may be permitted, the study of St. Patrick has been a lifelong preoccupation with me. In preparing this present work I have used principally: J. B. Bury, *The Life of St. Patrick*, London, 1904; Archbishop John Healy of Tuam, *The Life and Writings of St. Patrick*, Dublin, 1905; Eoin MacNeill, *St. Patrick, Apostle of Ireland*, New York, 1934; Ludwig Bieler,

The Life and Legend of St. Patrick, Dublin, 1948; Ludwig Bieler, *The Works* (literary) *of St. Patrick, St. Secundinus' Hymn on St. Patrick,* Westminster, (Maryland), London, England, 1953; Ludwig Bieler, *St. Patrick and the Coming of Christianity,* Dublin, 1967; The Thomas Davis Lectures, *St. Patrick,* especially the article of Rev. John Ryan, S.J., "The Traditional View" and the article of Rev. Paul Grosjean, S.J., "The Confession of St. Patrick," Dublin, 1958; Newport J. D. White, D.D., "The Hymn in Patrick's Praise by St. Sechnall," translated by Dr. White in his *The Writings of St. Patrick,* published by the Society for the Promotion of Christian Knowledge, London, 1932. (My thanks to the S. P. C. K. for permission to use the translation of this poem.) I have received and used many valuable ideas and excellent judgments from two brochures published by the *Irish Messenger:* Rev. Francis Shaw, S.J., *The Real St. Patrick,* Dublin, 1931; and Rev. P. J. Gannon, S.J., *Saint Patrick and the Irish Church,* Dublin, 1932. I wish to express my great gratitude to Rev. Paul Leonard, S.J., editor of the *Irish Messenger* for his generous permission allowing me the fullest use of both works.

For the English version of the *Confession* and the *Letter to the Soldiers of Coroticus* I translated the Latin texts found in Archbishop Healy's work. For the clarification of meanings I have consulted Dr. Healy's own translation, the translation of Dr. Newport J. D. White in his work, *The Latin Writings of St. Patrick,* published by the Royal Irish Academy, Dublin, 1905, and the recent translation of Dr. Ludwig Bieler. I have striven for a simple, literal translation, always saving clearness. St. Patrick himself insisted that he did not possess literary skill.

My special thanks is due to Rev. Carl Thayer, S.J., for reading, criticizing, and correcting the text, to Mrs. Helen Fitzgerald and Mrs. Barbara Titus for typing the entire work, to Thomas O'Connor, Ph.D., for drawing the two historical maps, and to James Murphy for the picture of St. Patrick's statue.

Martin P. Harney, S.J.
LECTURER IN IRISH HISTORY
BOSTON COLLEGE

WESTERN EUROPE
at the time of
SAINT PATRICK
Armagh
IRELAND
BRITAIN
Bannavem
Taberniae
Severn R.
Tours
Auxerre
Marmoutiers
GAUL
Lerins
Gorgonas
Capraria
Rome
SPAIN
ITALY
AFRICA
O'Connor

INTRODUCTION

The World of St. Patrick

The Roman Empire as it was existing in the last half of the fourth century and the first half of the fifth was the world of St. Patrick. It still extended over a vast territory, from Spain across to Syria, and from Britain down to North Africa. Its unity, however, was weakening; for a long time two divisions were forming. One was in the east, where the Greek language and thought predominated; this comprised Greece, the Balkans, Asia Minor, Syria, Palestine and Egypt, and its capital was Constantinople. The other was in the west, where the Latin language and thought were supreme; this included Italy, Illyricum, Gaul, Britain, Spain and Northern Africa, and its capital was nominally Rome but actually Milan. The divisions did not develop into separate empires; co-emperors ruled the two regions. Occasionally powerful personages, as Diocletian, Constantine and Theodosius, held both parts in overall dominion. St. Patrick was a man of the Latin west. He was born and reared in Britain, he spent many years as a monk in Gaul, and once at least he visited Italy. When Theodosius, the last emperor to rule the whole empire, died in 395, St. Patrick was then a lad of nine years.

The division of the empire grew out of the disasters which overwhelmed the Roman world in the third century. Political chaos, produced by chronic military revolts and civil wars, brought on general confusion and anarchy. From 192-284 twenty-five emperors ruled; their average rule was less than four years. Nearly all were raised by the praetorian guards, or by the legions; and nearly all were assassinated. Against the frontiers foreign invaders ominously marshalled their forces. In the east the Persians cut away four provinces. Along the Danube and the Rhine Teutonic tribes hammered at the defenses and twice penetrated them. In the northwest Irish and Picts, assailed by land and sea, isolated Britain. The dissolution of the Roman Empire seemed at hand.

That supreme catastrophe was averted by Diocletian, emperor from 285-305. A first class soldier, he had risen from the ranks to become one of the greatest of Rome's rulers. Born a Dalmatian peasant, he had little knowledge or appreciation of Roman traditions and institutions. His one desire was to save the empire; his single approach was the military commander's. Drastic were Diocletian's remedies: an imperial absolutism, unchecked by any institution whatsoever; a huge, highly-centralized bureaucracy that regulated in the minutest detail the lives of everyone in the empire, from patricians to slaves; and a mighty army of some 800,000 professional soldiers to uphold the establishment and to protect the frontiers. Both the enormous bureaucracy and the powerful army were placed completely under imperial control. Finally to finance this tremendous political and military machinery, and also to reverse the economic and social decline of the third century's chaos there was devised a gigantic and an inescapable taxation system.

Diocletian's program, and it was also his successors', was the only possible one for ending the existing anarchy. It did reestablish order, secured the frontiers and restored the economy —at least to the extent of supporting the bureaucracy and the army; and so it saved the empire politically for another hundred and fifty years. This was truly a formidable achievement; but it was about all that Diocletian and his successors accomplished. They failed lamentably to halt the economic, civic, social and cultural decline of the empire, especially in the Latin west, St. Patrick's world. Disasters piled upon disasters, until in 476 the Roman empire in the west was brought to an end.

The disintegration of the economy was caused largely by the massive taxation. Financing the bureaucracy and the army entailed the continual raising of enormous sums of money. Since the great nobles on their vast domains had achieved almost fiscal immunity, the tremendous sums could be obtained only by piling back-breaking taxes on the minor nobility, the bourgeoisie, the artisans and the peasants. The gravest hardships resulted for all these classes. The minor nobles not only had to pay heavy imposts, but they were ordered to collect the imposts of the other classes and to make up deficiencies from their own resources. The merchants were constantly threatened with bankruptcy, the artisans with impoverishment and the peasants with serfdom. In consequence the fourth and fifth centuries experienced no alleviation, but rather a multiplication of economic woes: monetary scarcity, compounded by the exhaustion of the mines; abandonment of large tracts of agricultural lands; restriction of manufactures and diminution of commerce.

This period of decline was also marked by the decay of civic government and of local political life. The Roman Empire at its peak was a confederation of over ten thousand cities, each one consisting of a walled urban center and the countryside around about it. Each city conducted its own political, economic and social life through a senate, modeled after Rome's, and called a *curia*. During the first two centuries this institution of self-government developed a class of skilled legislators and municipal officials. They were known as the *curiales.* In time they formed the local aristocracies. It might be said that, except for the remote provincial governors, the curiales of the Roman cities administered the internal affairs of the empire.

The importance of the cities waned in the fourth century. Already they had suffered much from the ravages of the civil wars, the abandonment of food-producing lands and the grave decline of the population caused by plagues and by pagan social vices. The new imperial bureaucracy through its hosts of administrators took over the municipal governments, with the consequent ruin of the local officialdoms. The plight of the curiales, ordered to collect heavy taxes and forced to make up deficiencies themselves, has already been noted. Some small aristocrats and merchants fled the cities to become farmers, even dependents of the great landowners. Others remained in the urban centers often to sink into the proletariat. The western half of the empire suffered the most in the decline of the cities.

As there seemed no halting of the disintegration, the imperial despotism, to guarantee the state against economic losses and social weaknesses, adopted the desperate expedient of locking Roman society into a caste-system. The stratification was made complete: occupations were declared hereditary, and all freedom of movement between the classes was stopped. For the curiales, the merchants, the artisans, the small landowners, the coloni and, even to an extent, the soldiers, there was no escape, especially after the imperial government had closed the Church, the army and the civil service to them. Discouragement and apathy ruled all. No wonder that there was little resistance to the barbarians when they came in the fifth century. This was the world of St. Patrick's youth.

One consequence of the decay of the cities was the decline of classical culture. The contemporary poverty precluded the construction of impressive public buildings; and a dying paganism offered little incentive for the erection of glorious temples. Similarly Latin literature experienced a decadence. The educated focused their literary interests on grammar, criticism, or imitation; a stilted oration, produced in oldtime pedantic rhetoric, was deemed the highest achievement. There was no creative writing. But here at least there was a new dawning; the rising Christianity had already been supplying cultural inspiration. In architecture the impressive basilica was being adapted for church buildings; and in art colorful mosaics were being employed for church adornment. A new literature too was appearing: the vigorously expressed thoughts of St. Ambrose, St. Jerome and St. Augustine, and the hymnody of Prudentius and St. Ambrose. These writers were all contemporaries of St. Patrick.

The fifth century brought to the western part of the Roman Empire its final disaster, the invasions of migrating Teutonic nations. These barbarian hordes, wherever they wandered, left behind them ravaged towns and countrysides. They added enormously to the already prevailing confusions, for they moved separately and not as units of a common Teutonic nationality. Such an idea was never dreamed of by them. Indeed for a century young Germans had been enlisting in the Roman armies. By the fifth century several legions were largely Teutonic, and some of the highest generals were Teutons. During the same period many thousands of Germans were settled as coloni within the frontiers. These soldiers and coloni remained loyal to Rome later in the invasions. The Latin provincials entertained no racial animosities against their Teutonic neighbors. Both suffered together in the catastrophes of the invasions. As for the migrating Teutons, they conquered different sections of the Roman territories; and on their conquests they established their own divergent kingdoms. Often they warred against each other, sometimes even as allies of the Roman emperors. In their new kingdoms the Teutonic wanderers were but a powerful military minority maintaining rule over a much more numerous population of quiescent Roman provincials.

The invasions of the Teutonic nations started in 376 and lasted for more than two centuries. St. Patrick lived within the first hundred years. In his boyhood and during his captivity in Ireland the Visigoths marched over Greece, Illyricum and northern Italy; the Alans, Burgundians,

Suevi and Vandals broke the barrier of the Rhine and swept over Gaul and Spain, and the Romans recalled their legions from Britain. In 410, the year of Patrick's escape, the Visigoths captured and sacked Rome. Patrick shared the consternation of all citizens of the empire at the incredible news. Three sovereignties divided Gaul while Patrick was there preparing himself as a monk and a cleric. They were: in the north an isolated Roman state, in the southeast the Kingdom of the Burgundians, and in the south and the southwest the Kingdom of the Visigoths. Roman generals governed the isolated fragment of the dying empire; the monarchs of the two kingdoms ruled over their own people as kings and over the Latin provincials as viceroys of the Roman emperor. In all three sovereignties the most important personages were the local bishops, for they had become the sole representatives of the provincial peoples with the kings and the generals. Both the Burgundians and the Visigoths were Arian heretics, and the Latin provincials were all Catholics. This difference proved an insurmountable barrier to amalgamation; it would only be leveled by the conversion of the Burgundians and the Visigoths in the sixth century.

The Roman world did not cease for Patrick when in 432 he left for his Irish mission. Always he would be an apostle of the Catholic religion, the religion held by all Romans and governed by the Pope of Rome. He ever remained keenly sensitive of his ties of blood and culture with

Britain and Gaul. When the harrowing reports reached him of the cruel massacres and the wholesale devastations perpetrated by the Huns in northern Gaul, by the Vandals in North Africa, and by the Saxons and Angles in Britain, he sorrowed with heartfelt sympathy for the Latin provincials overwhelmed in their frightful disasters.

Declining Roman society makes but half the story of the times in which St. Patrick lived. Growing Christianity completes the narrative. By the first half of the fifth century almost all Roman provincials were Christians; only in remote areas were pagans to be found. The authority of the Church now ran coextensively with the jurisdiction of the Empire. For that reason and also because of the new roles of the bishops as sole representatives of the people and as the saviors of Roman culture in the barbarian chaos, there developed in many minds a quasi-identification of Christianity with the Empire. Even when the imperial government faded away men still clung to the idea of a Roman world; and they found its bond of unity in Christianity.

In the contemporary world the leading personage was the pope. His prestige had grown as the understanding of his universal jurisdiction became more definite. From all parts appeals in disputes over dogma, discipline or jurisdiction came to him for his final decision. Of the nine popes who ruled during the lifetime of St. Patrick, St. Leo the Great, 440-461, illustrates best the increased importance of the Roman Pontiff. He dissuaded Attila the Hun from attacking Rome; and he successfully interceded for the people of Rome with Genseric the Vandal when the latter sacked the city. He negatived the claim of St. Hilary of Arles to consecrate the bishops of Vienne. He dealt firmly with widely scattered heretical groups, such as the Pelagians and Manichaeans in Italy and the Priscillianists in Spain. He opposed successfully the Monophysite heretics by his famous letter, the *Tome*, in which he vindicated the human nature of Jesus. The Council of Chalcedon accepted the *Tome* with the cry, "Peter hath spoken through Leo." It might also be remembered that St. Leo the Great in the first year of his pontificate officially approved of the faith of St. Patrick.

The bishops' leadership of the people and their preservation of culture has already been noted. But far more important, they were religious shepherds, teaching and ruling their flocks, guarding them against heresies, and promoting the conversion of the heathens. A large number of them are venerated as saints. By natural barriers and by the invasions they were hampered in their communications with Rome; often they had to act on their own initiative. But they were consistently loyal to the popes. Frequently the sovereign pontiffs made local bishops their special agents. The most renowned among the bishops was St. Germanus of Auxerre. He made his diocese the model see of Gaul and Britain. Twice he was sent by the popes to Britain to overcome the Pelagian heresy. It was under St. Germanus that St. Patrick was prepared for his apostolate.

One pressing concern of the bishops was the evangelization of the rural people; they were still largely heathen. Converting them was very difficult. The old Celtic heathenism was an amalgam of myths and superstitious rites tracing far back into prehistoric nature worship. It was entwined in every phase or happening of the peasants' lives; and they clung to it tenaciously. Intellectual appeals had small success in eradicating their ancient heathenish rites. Only the persistent zeal of apostolic heroes accomplished it. The first and greatest apostle of the rural people was St. Martin of Tours. During the twenty-six years of his episcopate, until his death in 397, he traversed tirelessly the countrysides of central Gaul from Tours to Auvergne, bringing the folk of the fields and the forests into the fold of Christ.

An especially vitalizing force in the contemporary Church was monasticism. First appearing in the west, in Italy, about 340, it spread rapidly there and through Gaul, Britain and Spain. The father of monasticism in Gaul was St. Martin of Tours. He founded several monasteries, the greatest of which was Marmoutier, situated but a few miles from his episcopal city. Two other important figures in Gallic monasticism were John Cassian, the founder of the monastery of St. Victor in Marseilles, and St. Honoratus, the founder of the monastery of Lerins, near the present Cannes. These two institutions continued for centuries to influence monastic life in the west. It is probable that St. Patrick visited Marmoutier. It is now accepted that he spent three years at Lerins and fifteen years at St. Germanus' monastery close to Auxerre. The monasteries of this period offered the Church a twofold service. First, they were the wellsprings of that spirituality which is supremely necessary for religious activities, and never more so than in chaotic times. The prayers and austerities of their monks and their nuns inspired all, cleric and layfolk, to the primary love and service of God; and they brought down the divine blessing and protection on all the Church's labors for God's kingdom. Secondly, these monasteries offered the Church rich sources for episcopal vocations. They have been termed seminaries for the future leaders of Christianity. St. Martin of Tours in his several monasteries, but above all in Marmoutier, produced many bishops and missionaries. His disciple, St. Ninian, the apostle of the North Britons, is a notable example. Lerins furnished the Church of Southern Gaul with many zealous and capable bishops and priests.

Much of ecclesiastical history in the fourth and fifth centuries was dominated by bitter disputes over Catholic doctrines. The period has been called "The Age of the Great Heresies." There were four great heresies, Arianism, Pelagianism, Nestorianism and Monophysitism, and several of lesser importance. Arianism, a denial of the divinity of the Second Person of the Trinity, was powerful in the east, owing to imperial support. It disappeared after its condemnation by the Council of Constantinople in 381; its greatest opponent was St. Athanasius. Arianism twice penetrated the west. It first appeared in the fourth century, backed by imperial pressure; but it was successfully opposed by St. Hilary of Poitiers and by St. Ambrose. It appeared again in the fifth century, but only as the national religion of the Teutonic conquerors; in consequence it had no appeal for the great bulk of the people, the Latin provincials. Their opposition was further strengthened by the occasional persecutions of the Arian Teutonic kings. Pelagianism, a denial of the necessity of God's grace for salvation, arose in the west about 400 and spread widely through the Latin world. It was refuted in masterful fashion by St. Augustine. After condemnations by local councils, by popes, and especially by the General Council of Ephesus in 431, Pelagianism disappeared.

Nestorianism and Monophysitism were heresies about the person and the natures of Jesus Christ. In origins and in progress both were almost entirely eastern. In the west, except for significant interventions of the popes, there was scarcely more than intense interest in these two fundamental controversies about the divinity and the humanity of the Savior. Both struggles were bitterly waged. Nestorianism, denying that Jesus was one person, maintained that there were present two distinct persons, a man and a god.

The Council of Ephesus officially condemned this proposition as heretical. St. Cyril of Alexandria was the outstanding opponent of Nestorianism. Monophysitism, swinging to the opposite extreme, taught that Jesus had only one nature, the divine, which had absorbed His human nature. The General Council of Chalcedon in 451 officially condemned this proposition as heretical. As has been noted earlier the Council of Chalcedon enthusiastically accepted the *Tome* of St. Leo in which the great pope clearly explained the Catholic doctrine with this statement: "The One Person of our Lord possesses two natures, the Divine and the Human, neither confused nor mixed."

The fourth and fifth centuries have also been named "The Age of the Great Fathers." The fathers were early ecclesiastical writers, men of deep learning, orthodoxy in doctrine and sanctity of life, who witnessed to, interpreted and defended the uninterrupted tradition of the Church. Fashioned in the old classical culture, by their own lofty, forceful and brilliant writings they were also the creators of the new Christian literature. The period of the Fathers' greatest activity came between the Council of Nicaea in 325 and the Council of Chalcedon in 451, the very time of the great heresies. In no other period of her history has the Church had so many and such brilliant champions.

It was providential for St. Patrick that he was a contemporary, or a near-contemporary, of the great fathers: St. Athanasius, St. Hilary of

Poitiers, St. Basil, St. Gregory of Nyssa, St. Ephraem, St. Cyril of Jerusalem, St. Gregory Nazianzen, St. Ambrose, St. John Chrysostom, St. Jerome, St. Augustine, St. Cyril of Alexandria, St. Peter Chrysologus, St. Prosper of Aquitaine and Pope St. Leo I. The span of his life corresponded with the last third of the great patristic period. Because of that fact, some of the fathers were dead when St. Patrick was born, and several others had died before he departed from Gaul. A few survived until the ending of his Irish apostolate. Whether the fathers were living or dead, their writings and their deeds would offer most effective inspiration. Patrick, because of his inadequate intellectual attainments, could not gain a wide acquaintance with patristic writings; but his monastic training, devoted studying of Holy Scripture and close attention to his preceptors in their instructions on the Faith furnished him with a practical knowledge of patristic ideals.

On the summit of Patrick's world stood Christ's Church. In consequence the Fathers, as her champions against the heresies, were his heroes. Necessarily they were far distant from him. But he had other religious heroes, much closer to him, the missionary saints who brought Christ's Church to rural heathens. One of these was his bishop, St. Germanus of Auxerre, and another was the apostle of the northern Britons, St. Ninian. But preeminently above all was the patriarchal St. Martin of Tours. These were the exemplars that sustained him during the years of preparation for the long-prayed-for apostolate.

For almost half a century, except for the six years of his captivity in Ireland, St. Patrick's world was limited by the boundaries of the Roman Empire. In 432 came a change, and for the next thirty years, until his death, Patrick's world converged on Ireland. Those three decades were the most important in his life, for they witnessed the conversion of the Irish people. This Ireland of his apostolate differed from the Gaul of his preparation in almost every feature: history, traditions, language, culture, organization and religion. The reason for the diversity was that Ireland had never been a part of the Roman Empire, and hence had never been Latinized. It is not to be thought that the Irish lived in complete isolation from Roman influence. They maintained many trading-contacts. In the fourth and fifth centuries, the days of imperial decline, Irish kings ravaged the west coasts of Roman Britain and established petty kingdoms there. The raiders who returned brought back British Christians to be sold into slavery in Ireland. One such slave was St. Patrick.

Ireland is a compact island with an area of 32,000 miles. Mountain ranges, steep-sloped but of no great height, fringe almost its entire coastline of 2,100 miles and encircle its great central plain. This plain for the most part is fertile, though it contains wide stretches of bog-lands; it is dotted with numerous lakes and is crossed by several rivers. In ancient times, and until four centuries ago, the island was thickly forested. The population of Ireland at the advent of St. Patrick would be hard to estimate; a figure of around 300,000 would be only a very hazardous guess. Two things are certain: the population was of very ancient origins and was of very mixed character. Archaeologists have found traces of mesolithic hunters, of neolithic builders of stone tombs and cromlechs, and of bronze-age artificers and herdsmen. The peoples of the bronze-age, short in stature and swarthy in complexion, dominated the land for centuries and centuries. In the early part they were the pre-Aryan Firbolgs, and in the later part they were the Picts, pre-Aryans too with possible Celtic admixtures. The descendants of the Firbolgs and the Picts constituted the majority of the people of the island in the fifth century A.D.; and evidences of them are still discernible in the North and West of Ireland today.

Finally, about 350 B.C., the last immigrants arrived in the land. They were of the Celtic race, the Aryan (Indo-European) people who at the time dominated western Europe. They called themselves Gaels and their language, which was akin to the speech of the Celts of Gaul and Britain, Gaelic. They were of great stature, ruddy complexion, and hair red or brown. They bore weapons of iron; and they were the first men of the Iron Age to appear in Ireland. These Gaels were warlike, aristocratic and masterful; and they had invaded Ireland with the intent to conquer it. Tall and powerful fighting men wielding iron swords and spears, they crushed their bronze-age adversaries. So complete was their conquest that, though they remained an upper-class minority, they imposed their language, customs and law upon the vanquished. Yet for the new Irish nation which they created they borrowed much from the very ancient culture of the older peoples. Their bards took over the old traditions, myths and legends, first putting them into Gaelic in oral form, and then, when writing came in the fifth century A.D., transmitting the spoken Gaelic accounts to the pages of permanent manuscripts. Thus the cultural traditions of the ancient races of the land had become the culture of the newly fused Irish nation. Professor Curtis well remarked that the traditions of the Irish people are the oldest of any European race north or west of the Alps. St. Patrick during the years of his apostolate undoubtedly would recognize divergencies; but he would be more impressed with the unities. His flock considered themselves Celts, they held a common culture, they conversed in a common Gaelic language. The Romans could call them by the common names of Hibernians, or Scoti; but the inhabitants of Ireland knew one another as Gaels.

The political organization of Ireland in St. Patrick's day consisted of seven major kingdoms. They were Ulster, Leinster, Meath, Oriel, Aileach, Connacht and Munster. Ulster occupied the northeast corner (the present Antrim and Down). It was the oldest kingdom, and at one time controlled most of the north (the present Ulster). Leinster was in the southeast and embraced much of the present Leinster south of

Dublin and Meath. Its chief seat was at Ferns. Meath stretched from the Shannon eastward to the Irish Sea and included the present northern counties of Leinster. Its chief seat was at Tara. Oriel ran from Dundalk to Sligo and covered the modern Monaghan, Armagh, Fermanagh, and possibly a part of Sligo. Aileach occupied all of the north from the Bann River westward to the Atlantic, the area of the present Tyrone, Derry and Donegal. Its chief seat was near Derry, the Grianan of Aileach. There were two great divisions of Aileach, Tir-Eoghan (Tyrone) and Tir-Chonaill (Donegal). Connacht, almost as ancient as Ulster and Leinster, embraced all the area of the present province of Connacht, with the addition of Cavan. Its chief seat was at Cruachan. Munster included the whole of the south from Leinster west to the Atlantic (the present province of Munster). Its seat was at Cashel. Two powerful groups divided Munster, the Eoghanactha in the center and the Dal Chais in the west.

Four of the kingdoms owed their foundation to Niall of the Nine Hostages (379-405) or to his family. Meath, his own kingdom, he raised to supreme importance at Tara. Oriel was established with his assistance. Aileach was created by two of his sons. Connacht was founded by two of his brothers. The kings (ris) of Meath, Aileach and Connacht were to rule successively at Tara as High King (Ard Ri). The High-Kingship was little more than a title of prestige and of precedence at the rare national gatherings. It was only fully acknowledged in the four kingdoms of the family of Niall. Even in these the actual power of the high-king was restricted to his own state. The kings of Ulster and Leinster were often hostile; and the kings of Munster were engrossed in extending their own position at Cashel.

Under each of the major kingdoms there were numerous petty kingdoms. In the whole of Ireland they totaled over one hundred and eighty. The Gaelic word for them was *tuath,* i.e a population group capable of maintaining 3,000 or less (down to 700) soldiers in emergency. By extension, *tuath* also meant the land occupied by the group. The *tuath* was usually called a kingdom and its ruler a *ri* (king). The functions of these petty kings were similar to those of the major kings; they governed their states, presided over the assemblies of the freemen and led the soldiers in war. The tributes which they received and the favors which they granted were on a smaller scale than what they in turn gave and received from the major kings. All rights and duties of the various political groups were carefully regulated by old customs, which about the time of St. Patrick were committed to writing in the *Book of Rights.* An ancient tradition attributes the *Book of Rights* to St. Benignus, first Irish disciple and first successor of St. Patrick.

Fifth-century Ireland's economy and social system were wholly rural, and based completely on agriculture and grazing. There were no cities at all, although the habitations clustering around great seats like Tara or Cashel would bear resemblance to small medieval towns, especially during large popular assemblies and fairs. Everything was paid for in kind; cattle, horses, silverware or iron implements. Whatever hard money there was came by the way of foreign commerce. No great roads like those of the Romans crossed the country.

There were five social classes: (1) kings, (2) nobles, (3) freemen with property, (4) freemen without property, and (5) the non-free people. The latter class included absolute slaves, others not much better off, and some far above slavery. Professional men, such as physicians, bards, historians, brehons (judges) and artificers were given the status of freemen. Bards were rather genealogists and historians than poets in the modern sense, though there were some of these.

After the kings one of the most influential groups were the brehons. They were the judges who interpreted the ancient laws of Ireland and adjudicated the cases arising under the law. Some were attached to the courts of the kings; others, unattached, arbitrated the disputes submitted by private litigants. Eventually the interpretations and the numerous laws hardened into a great code which came to be called the Brehon Laws. Probably the Brehon Laws were written down about St. Patrick's time, when writing was introduced into Ireland. The *Seanchus Mor*, the great collection, seems to reach back to his period. The Brehon Laws affected every phase of Irish life. They regulated all ranks of society, as well as all the rights and duties involved; they furnished minute rules for the conduct of property, industries and evidence; they arranged the relations between all classes of the people; they even established the fees of professional men. The Brehon Laws were unlike the Roman Code which was statute law; and they were also unlike the English Common Law which was a combination of Anglo-Saxon customs and canon law. Rather they were the decisions and opinions of skilled judges in the light of the ancient laws of Ireland on the issues submitted to them. The Brehon Laws affected nearly every question that could arise.

Probably for St. Patrick the most distinctive feature of Ireland in 432 was its heathenism. Many were the pagan gods worshipped there. The Gaels brought with them the Celtic deities of Gaul; and they mixed the veneration of them with the ancient tribal cults of the original peoples. Religious honors were paid to the memories of dead ancestors. Such commemorations were striking features of the great assemblies like the Aonach of Tailteann and the Aonach of Carman, both of which were held in cemeteries. The countrysides were filled with sacred places of the dead. A very important place in Irish paganism was given to the worship of the forces of nature: the sun, light, fire and water, but especially the sun. Religious festivals were held to mark the change of the seasons. Idols of stone also were worshipped; the best known was Crom Cruach and its ring of twelve smaller idols at Magh Sleacht (in the present Cavan). As with all rural paganism the thoughts and activities of the people of Ireland were enslaved by countless and deeply-rooted superstitions.

The heathen religion of the Irish people has often been designated *Druidism,* owing to the prominence of druids in their Gaelic paganism. And yet, the druids, neither in Ireland, nor in Britain, nor in Gaul, were priests. They were not offerers of the sacrificial worship. They were, as they claimed to be, masters and teachers of higher learning, especially of occult sciences and of doctrines about the supernatural world and its inhabitants. They were considered to be magicians, augurs, who foretold future events, and soothsayers. And they were believed to possess powers of enchantment and of casting spells. The druids were numerous in Ireland, highly reputed, and yet greatly feared. To their credit it should be said that they kept alive the legends and epic tales of Irish tradition. This was a tremendous task; it meant the exact memorizing of countless lines of oral poetry, for as yet there was not any writing in Ireland. Many of the druids accepted Christianity at St. Patrick's coming, though some remained bitterly hostile to the end. But St. Patrick did not abolish the druidical order; he sought to Christianize it. The converted druids changed their appellation to *filidh* (in Latin, *poetae;* in English, poets). Actually the filidh were philosophers more than poets. When writing became common the filidh cooperated with the monks in committing the ancient heroic tales to permanent manuscripts. The filidh also conducted the Bardic Schools, where the Gaelic language, literature and history were preserved down to the seventeenth century.

This was the Irish world in 432, when St. Patrick stepped from his small boat onto the shore of Strangford Lough in County Down. For the next thirty years this Ireland would be the land of his apostolate. During those decades there would be no change in its physical aspects, in its governmental structure, in its social system and in its economy. But there would be a tremendous change in its people, almost the whole of them would have become Christian, and with such deep conviction that their faith would become proverbial. This was St. Patrick's accomplishment.

IRELAND
in the days of
ST. PATRICK
Dal Riada
Cineal Chonaill
Aileach
Slemish Mt.
AILEACH
Cineal Eoghan
ULAIDH
Armagh
OIRGHIALLA
Saul
Feara Manach
Briefne
Dal
Ui Briuin
Ui Fiachrach
Cruachan
Tara
CRUACHAN
TARA
Conmaicne
Cianachta
Lambay Is.
Delvins
Ui Maine
Ui Failghe
Ui Murray
Thomond
Dal Chais
Ossory
LAIGHIN
Ferns
Cashel
Ciarraidhe
Ui Cinnsealaigh
CAISEAL
Eoghanachta
Deisi
Desmond
Corca Dhuibhne
Muscraidhe
Corca Luighe
O'Connor

The Career of St. Patrick

A brief account of St. Patrick's life is called for in a study of his two authentic writings. It is well to keep in mind the difficulties involved in any telling of St. Patrick's story. Biographical data are scarce, only a few facts mentioned vaguely in the *Confession* and the *Letter*—and even the meaning of these incidents has been endlessly debated. The two earliest biographies, Muirechu's and Tirechan's, both written two hundred years after St. Patrick's death, go back to his day largely through traditions. Lives of saints produced abundantly in Ireland from the tenth to the twelfth centuries possess little historical value. The authors exaggerated the glory of their saintly heroes, using miraculous tales beyond all reason. What kernels of truth these works may have contained were buried under their extravagances. These extravagances persisted down through the centuries, and even still find much usage among writers and orators. They are among the chief sources for the false image of St. Patrick so prevalent today. The person of the saint also has been obscured by recent disputes over the possibility of two Patricks. However, the majority of scholars[1] of Early Irish Church History accept the one St. Patrick, the author of the *Confession* and the *Letter*, and the one Apostle of Ireland. A striking paradox exists in St. Patrick's life-story: there is a paucity of factual details, and yet an abundance of self-revelations. After all, he was not writing an autobiography, but a defense of himself and his apostolate.

St. Patrick was born about 385 in Roman Britain at a small place called Bannavem Taberniae. His father, an official of the town, lived at a villa in its vicinity. The location of Bannavem Taberniae has long been debated. Nowadays most Patrician scholars favor a site near the shore of the estuary of the Severn River. The father's name was Calpornius. He was a decurion, that is, a member of the local curia which administered the town's affairs and collected the taxes—with the responsibility of personally making up the deficits. Calpornius' position indicates that

[1]Among these scholars may be mentioned Professor Eoin MacNeill, Father John Ryan, S.J., Père Paul Grosjean, S.J., and Professor Ludwig Bieler.

he was somewhat wealthy and that also he was a nobleman. Patrick speaks of the manservants and the maidservants of his father's house. He writes explicitly of his social rank: "I was born of a father who was a decurion. But I sold my nobility, I blush not to state it, nor am I sorry, for the profit of others." The mother's name was Concessa; but of her nothing historically certain is known. Patrick declares that his paternal grandfather, Potitus, was a priest. This fact is interesting, because it was about this time that the discipline of celibacy was being introduced into the Latin Church.

In describing his boyhood Patrick disparagingly portrays himself as a wayward youth, the associate of a group of like scatterbrains who were ignorant of God, disobedient to the commandments and heedless of their priests. Whatever Patrick's faults were, it should be remembered that he penned this severe indictment many years afterwards and from the standpoint of a very austere monk, trained to despise not only the vices, but the frivolities of the decadent Roman society. He sharply criticized too his youthful carelessness in secular education. But Patrick overstated his negligences. The schools of Rhetoric of his day aimed not so much at familiarizing the students with the masterpieces of Latin Literature as at enabling them to speak classical Latin, even in the ordinary affairs of their everyday lives. This was a hard enough task for youths in Italy or Gaul. How difficult it must have been for a lad in remote Britannia, the least Romanized portion of the western empire. Slave-raiders from Ireland ended the puzzlements of Patrick's schooldays.

In the fourth century Roman Britain was invaded time and again by piratical raids from Ireland. Towards the end, under Niall of the Nine Hostages, the High-King, the raids grew into large expeditions. They inflicted wholesale devastations on the towns and the countrysides; and they carried off numerous prisoners as slaves. In the last of these expeditions Patrick was captured at his father's villa. The year was 401, and the lad was about sixteen. With a large crowd of prisoners he was transported to Ireland to be sold into slavery.

Patrick's master was Miliucc, a petty king, ruling in the northeast corner of Ireland (in the center of the present County Antrim). The north of his territory was dominated by Slemish Mountain, 1,437 feet. On this mountain the new slave boy had to toil, tending his master's flocks, the swine in the woods at its foot and the sheep on its higher slopes. It was the loneliest of tasks, for the lad had with him not a single companion of his own race and faith.

Yet it was in the solitudes of Slemish that the Christian teachings of his parents and his priests reasserted themselves. Patrick renewed his practices of prayer. In the *Confession* he decribes the holy vigils of his slave days:

Now after I came to Ireland I herded flocks; and often during the day I prayed. The love of God and the fear of Him increased more and more, and my faith grew, and my spirit was stirred up, so that in a single day I said as many as a hundred prayers, and at night nearly as many, even when I was out in the woods and on the mountain. Before the dawn I used to arouse myself to prayer in snow and frost and rain; and I minded no pain, nor was there any sluggishness in me, as now I feel, because the spirit was fervent within me.

Further, he chastened his will and strengthened his soul by enduring the hardships and the humiliations of his servitude. It surely can be said that Patrick, all alone on Slemish Mountain, made there his first novitiate.

Besides the spiritual renewal Patrick mentions but one other fact of his captive years, his acquiring the Gaelic language. When he arrived in Ireland he was a Latin-speaker, with possibly some ability in the tongue of the Celtic Britons. Circumstances forced him to become a Gaelic-speaker. He must have obtained a practical usage of the language of Ireland, for on his return in 432, after an absence of twenty-four years, he was able to resume the Gaelic speech. Though no other experiences are noted, Patrick must have achieved a considerable knowledge of the character, ideas and customs of the Irish people. Certainly he gained a deep, abiding love for them. Later he was able so to identify himself with his flock that he appears in history almost as an Irishman.

After he had been captive for six years, one night in his sleep he heard a voice saying, "Thou fastest well; soon thou wilt go to thy fatherland." Patrick usually spoke of his heavenly messages as coming to him in dreams; legends later magnified them into the words of a special angel. After a short time, again he heard the heavenly voice; this time it said, "Lo, thy ship is ready." Its location was not at hand, but about two hundred miles away. Patrick had never been in the region, nor did he know any person there. Nevertheless, trusting in God, he took up his flight. The place was probably on the southeastern coast, in the present County Wexford.

When Patrick arrived the ship was just about to sail. Its cargo was Irish wolfhounds, then popular on the continent. The crew were all Irish pagans. Patrick asked to be allowed to work his passage. The captain sharply and indignantly refused his request. The lad, sorely discouraged, but praying fervently turned back to his lodging. But the shout of a sailor recalled him. The captain and the crew had changed; they were now willing to take him. So Patrick sailed with them to Gaul.

After three days they made land. Then they journeyed for twenty-eight days through a desert where they did not meet a single soul. This "desert" was the devastated and depopulated land of northern Gaul. Shortly before, the region had been ravaged by the fierce Vandals and Alans, following their smashing of the Rhine defenses. In the lonely solitudes the situation of Patrick's party grew hopeless; their food was failing and death from starvation was threatening them. The despairing captain challenged Patrick, the Christian, to pray to his all-powerful God to save them. Patrick did so. And also he urged the pagan sailors to turn to God and to beg Him to send them food on that very day. In the *Confession* Patrick writes that shortly they came upon a herd of wild swine from which the starving men obtained enough meat for themselves and their hounds to last them until their destination was reached.

It seens likely that soon after his first venturings in Gaul Patrick returned to his home and parents. "And once more, after a few years, I was in Britain with my family. They received me as a son and earnestly besought me that now at least, after so many tribulations which I had undergone, I should never depart from them." Professor MacNeill believes that "a few years" would be largely accounted for by the six years of the captivity. He points out too that the first revelation which Patrick received, "soon thou wilt go to they fatherland," would be for Patrick a command no less than a prophecy. The words, "They received me as a son," mean, according to Professor MacNeill, that Patrick was given his rightful place in the family. The earnest pleas to him never to leave again only added emphasis. Later on in the *Confession* Patrick recalls these strong desires of his parents and his family: "And many gifts were offered to me with weeping and tears...It was not my grace, but God who conquered in me, and withstood them all, so that I came to the Irish tribes to preach the Gospel."

It was while he was in Britain that Patrick received the definite call for his Irish apostolate.

And there indeed I saw in a vision of the night a man whose name was Victoricus coming as it were from Ireland with countless letters. He gave me one of them, and I read the beginning of the letter, which was entitled, 'The Voice of the Irish.' And whilst I was reading aloud the beginning of the letter, I thought that at that very moment I heard the voices of those who dwelt beside the Wood of Foclut, which is nigh unto the Western Sea. And thus they cried, as with one mouth, 'We beseech thee, holy youth, to come and walk once more amongst us.' And I was exceedingly touched in my heart, and could read no more, and so I awoke. Thanks be to God, after many years the Lord granted to them according to their earnest cry.

The vision meant for Patrick but one thing, that God was calling him to be a missionary to the pagan Irish. But he was not a man to move rashly. Two other mystical experiences finally convinced him. He summarized their conclusions by borrowing words from St. John and from St. Paul: "He who laid down his life for thee, He it is who speaketh in thee" (1 John 3:16); "The Spirit helpeth the infirmities of our prayer" (Rom. 8:26); and "The Lord our Advocate maketh intercession for us" (1 John 2:1). He no longer held back.

To prepare himself Patrick set out for the monasteries of Gaul. There, following the practice of the times, he moved about from one center of holy learning to another. To trace his course is difficult. He must early have visited Tours, if only to seek inspiration at the tomb of St. Martin, who had died but ten years before. Patrick says definitely that he visited the monks and the hermits who dwelt on the Italian islands of the Tyrrhenian Sea. It is certain that he stayed at the monastery of Lerins, off the southeast coast of Gaul, possibly for three years. There he lived under the guidance of its holy abbot, St. Honoratus, one of the fathers of western monasticism. Finally Patrick came to the monastery of Auxerre; and there for a decade and a half he prayed and lábored under the supervision of its holy founder, St. Germanus. The experiences Patrick gained were later to be invaluable in his own episcopacy in Ireland. St. Germanus of Auxerre was the greatest bishop in northern Gaul. He was the pope's special representative; twice he was sent by Pope St. Celestine into Britain to overcome the Pelagian heresy. It was St. Germanus who subsequently consecrated Patrick a bishop.

During the years of preparation Patrick strove for two objectives. First he sought personal sanctity. Faithfully following the daily routine of prayer and penance at Lerins and Auxerre he grew in remarkable holiness. Secondly he labored to acquire solid priestly knowledge. This goal meant for the former slave continual discouragement, so meagre was his preparation—only the confused memories of his neglectful schooldays. Patrick never became a learned ecclesiastic. Moreover, he was primarily a man of action, with little inclination for intellectual achievements. His writings are but very modest endeavors. And yet these writings reveal one thing, his truly remarkable familiarity with Holy Scripture. In the *Confession*, a pamphlet of twenty-one pages, and in the *Letter*, a pamphlet of seven pages, he embodied in the texts no fewer than 190 quotations from the Sacred Writings. Evidently here he made good, practical use of the monastic education of his day, which was largely based on the Holy Scriptures. Long and hard were the years of his preparation; but through them all Patrick faithfully kept in his heart his desire one day to convert the people of Ireland.

In 429, finally, the conversion of the Irish came under the consideration of St. Germanus, during his first mission in Britain. One of his tasks was the improvement of conditions in the British church. For this purpose he held local gatherings of bishops and clerics to confer with him and the Gaulish priests who were assisting him. At one of these meetings the project of a mission to Ireland was put forth. There were Irish settlements in the western regions (the present Wales and Cornwall), and there were numberless British Christian slaves in Ireland. For the leadership of this mission Patrick's name and qualifications were discussed. At the time Patrick was in Gaul and knew nothing about the project. He was later told about it; and he was also told that a very dear friend of his had strongly advocated his cause. This same friend went further; he intimated to Patrick that he was to be made a bishop.

In 430 a second conference about the Irish mission was held, this time at Auxerre. It was far more important. Patrick himself was present. The superior clergy were to make the decision. Their vote was favorable; and so the mission to Ireland was instituted. Strangely Patrick makes no mention of this fact, so important in the history of his apostolate. Perhaps he felt that his readers were familiar with the decision. Instead Patrick describes the painful humiliations which he had to suffer during the proceedings of the conference. There was strong opposition to his being made a bishop. He was declared to be only half-educated, uncultured, slow and hesitant of speech. He was labeled a visionary, a self-seeker, a rash fellow who rushed heedlessly into the gravest dangers. It was strongly protested that he, an unworldly monk, was no person to be a missionary bishop in a heathen land, where the Church was not even established. The cruelest blow came when his "friend" about-faced and revealed to the superior clergy a grave sin which Patrick committed when he was a boy of fifteen. Patrick had confessed the sin before he was raised to the diaconate. But later on he was so plagued by the memory of it that, for the peace of his soul, he revealed it in confidence to this friend. Patrick in sorrow writes: "He put me to shame publicly before everyone, good or bad." The revelation was decisive, and Patrick was rejected.

Patrick's reprobation—"reprobation" was the very word he used—overwhelmed him completely. All his hopes and plans of twenty years vanished. His world collapsed about him. In total dejection he was tempted to despair. He wrote: "Truly on that day I was so cast down that I might have fallen here and in eternity." But

Patrick was a man of faith, and recovery came quickly to him. He notes in the *Confession* that on that very night by a vision God comforted and strengthened him, and restored his confidence. In glowing terms he thanked God. Patrick forgave his rejectors and prayed for them, even for the "friend" who had abused his confidence.

St. Palladius, the promoter of St. Germanus' journey into Britain, was chosen to head the mission to Ireland. Pope Celestine consecrated him a bishop and sent him "to the Irish who believe in Christ." Palladius reached Ireland in 431. After a short stay, during which he established a few churches in Leinster, in the same year, he departed for Britain most likely to seek priests for his mission. But before the year was out St. Palladius died in Britain.

Meanwhile in Gaul Patrick's humble submission was being noted. Many began to form more favorable opinions of him. St. Germanus, especially, trusted him; after Patrick's ordination to the priesthood the great bishop of Auxerre sent him to the assistance of Palladius in Ireland. To bear witness that the new priest now was going to Ireland with the approval and on the command of his superiors, St. Germanus ordered Segitius, an elder priest, to accompany him. Patrick was overjoyed by such a justification. "And my faith has been approved before God and man," he wrote.

As Patrick and his companion were journeying from Auxerre to Ireland, on the road near Evreux, they met clerics returning from

Ireland, bearing the news that St. Palladius was dead. At once they turned back to Auxerre and to St. Germanus, the papal representative for the mission to Ireland. The great bishop now was convinced that Patrick was the chosen one of God to be the apostle of the Irish nation. Accordingly St. Germanus consecrated him a bishop in 432. Not long afterwards, in that same year of 432, Bishop Patrick sailed to Ireland. His ship, moving up the east coast, eventually entered Strangford Lough, an arm of the Irish Sea that stretches northward twenty miles through what is now County Down. On the lough's southern shore Patrick built his settlement. It was in the district ruled by Dichu, a scion of the kings of Ulaidh, the most ancient line of Irish royalty. Dichu welcomed Patrick, listened to him and was baptized by him; probably he was the saint's first Irish convert. In gratitude Dichu presented to his father-in-God a piece of land and a large barn that stood upon it. This structure St. Patrick made his first church in Ireland. *Sabhall Padraig* (the barn of Patrick) it came to be known; and its memory is still preserved in the village of Saul which marks its site. The Gaelic pronunciation is "Saul Padraig."

The difficulties attending the writing of a biographical sketch of St. Patrick have already been cited: the paucity of details in Patrick's writings; the lateness of the first biographies, written more than two centuries after his death and tracing their accounts back through legends to the incidents of his life; and the large amount of extravagant medieval traditions. However, there are some far more sound authorities; they are the medieval chronicles, the *Annals of Tighernach* and the *Annals of Ulster*. In these chronicles the events of Patrick's mission are stated briefly and without exaggerations. They are highly regarded by Doctor Bury. The events concerning St. Patrick's mission are thus listed:

A.D. 431. The mission of Palladius.
A.D. 432. Patrick arrived in Ireland.
A.D. 439. Secundinus, Auxilius and Iserninus, themselves also bishops, were sent to Ireland to the aid of Patrick.
A.D. 441. Leo ordained Bishop of Rome and Patrick the Bishop was approved in the Catholic Faith. In the *Annals of Innisfallen:* The probation[1] of St. Patrick in the Catholic Faith.
A.D. 443. Patrick the Bishop flourishing in the ardor of faith and the doctrine of Chirst in our province.
A.D. 444. Ard Macha[2] was founded.
A.D. 447. Death of St. Secundinus in the seventy-fifth year of his age.
A.D. 459. Auxilius the Bishop died.

---

[1]"Probation" here means "approbation," possibly after examination.

[2]Ard Macha: in English, Armagh.

A.D. 461. The death of Patrick.
A.D. 468. Iserninus died.

The third of these dates reveals the early success of St. Patrick's mission. After the first seven years, during which he was the only bishop, the numbers of the Christians were such that three assistant bishops were sent to him. Auxilius and Iserninus had been companions of Patrick at Auxerre, under the direction of St. Germanus. Secundinus was from Gaul, and probably also from Auxerre. He was to become the next in importance to Patrick in the primitive Irish Church. To Secundinus is credited a long poem in praise of Patrick, composed during the saint's lifetime. Patrick assigned his assistant bishops to the following localities: he gave Secundinus a place not far from Tara, the residence of the High-King; he gave Auxilius a place near Naas, the residence of the kings of northern Leinster; and he gave to Iserninus a place near Aghade on the river Slaney, in the lands of the king of southern Leinster.

Patrick, Secundinus, Auxilius, and Iserninus are considered the authors of the earliest collection of canons for the government of the Irish Church. One of these canons, cited in the *Book of Armagh,* indicates the Catholicity of the Irish Church. It decrees that problems which cannot be solved on the local level are to be referred to the bishop of Armagh, and in the event that he cannot solve them, they are to be referred to Rome. The salutation opening another very early collection of canons bears considerable significance. It goes thus: "We give thanks to God the Father, and the Son, and the Holy Spirit. To the priests, deacons and all the clergy, Patricius, Auxilius, Iserninus, bishops, greetings." Since it does not carry the name of Secundinus, it may be dated after his death in 447. Further, the document is not addressed to any other bishops, who would have to be mentioned, if there were such. From these two collections of canons it may be assumed that Patrick was the only bishop in Ireland during the first seven years of his mission, and also that there were only the four named until sometime after the death of Secundinus.

The geographical positions of the first four episcopal sees are of great importance. They indicate the progress of Patrick's mission; and they reveal the first steps for the organization of the Irish Church on a territorial basis. Patrick founded his own see at Armagh, and gave to it the primacy of Ireland. Throughout all his writings Patrick never ceased maintaining that he, and he alone, was the chief pastor of the Irish Church. The location of his see indicates that by 444, when Armagh was founded, Patrick's mission extended through a large part of the present province of Ulster. Undoubtedly, Patrick was moved to choose the site of Armagh (Ard Macha, in Gaelic) because of its proximity to Eamhain Macha, the most famous settlement of Irish saga literature. In the legends the kings of Eamhain Macha rule over the entire North; a few legends even present them as dominating much of the rest of Ireland. Long before St. Patrick's time Eamhain Macha's power had disappeared. But the memories about its mighty monarch, Connor MacNessa, remained with the Irish people. The earthworks of his Eamhain Macha still stand, even in our day, about a mile and a half from Armagh. The see of Secundinus, but a few miles from Tara, afforded him contact with the High-King of Ireland, who reigned directly over Meath and indirectly over Oriel, Aileach, and Connacht. Auxilius' see at Naas placed him near the ruler of northern Kildare; and Iserninus' see not more than a two hour journey from Rathvilly, placed him near the chief king of Leinster. In this location of the seats of ecclesiastical government near to the seats of secular government, Patrick and his assistant bishops were acting in accord with the general policy of the Church of their times.

The location of the four Irish bishoprics would seem to indicate that Patrick's apostolate, during much of its early years, was chiefly successful in the eastern half of Ireland. This, of course, does not preclude fruitful missionary journeys into the west and the south. Besides his direct apostolate Patrick must have been busily engaged, during those first years, in training priest-assistants from Britain and Gaul in the Irish language and customs. Certainly he devoted himself to forming a native clergy solidly taught and firmly disciplined. His first successor in the see of Armagh was an Irishman,

St. Benignus (Benin), who as a young boy was one of Patrick's first converts at Saul.

Professor Bury makes much of a statement in the *Annals of Ulster* that in the year 441, the year in which St. Leo the Great became pope, Patrick was approved in the Faith. The poem of St. Secundinus may contain a reference to it in the line where Patrick is said to be "Testis Domini fidelis in lege catholica" (Faithful witness of the Lord in the Catholic law). Bury connects the statement in the *Annals of Ulster* with an Irish tradition of Patrick visiting Rome and bringing back to Armagh relics of the apostles, Peter and Paul, and of the martyrs, Stephen and Lawrence. He then infers that Patrick at this stage of his mission (441-442), having in mind the establishment of Armagh as a metropolitan see, desired to seek approval of his work, his teachings and his plans from the highest authority in Christendom, and this by a personal visit to the Apostolic See. However, though Patrick's visit to Rome is highly probable, it cannot be fully established on the evidence that is now at hand. A contrary argument, drawn from Patrick's assertion in the *Confession* that he dared not leave his flock, even to visit his kindred in Britain or to see again the holy companions of his monastic days in Gaul, has little weight. The remark referred to his own personal pleasure. There is nothing in Patrick's declaration that precluded an official visit to the Apostolic See of Rome in the interests of his mission or the spiritual welfare of his flock.

Listing St. Patrick's missionary activities according to place and time is extremely difficult. Studying his apostolic methods is more rewarding; and it is easier, because it can be made by perusing the texts of his two writings. One summary of his labors is especially striking:

> I journeyed for your sake through many places, even where no man dwelt, and where never had anyone come to baptize, or to ordain clergy, or to confirm the people. I have, by the bounty of God the Lord, done everything carefully and most gladly for your salvation.

It must be remembered that Patrick began his mission after he had passed middle life. He describes himself as being at that time a worn-out man. Well he might have been after years of following the rigorously penitential rules of the monasteries of Gaul. The quotation above is then a portrayal of the painstaking toils of an aging shepherd through thirty years, traversing the never-ending roads, penetrating into the deep forests and struggling up the steep mountain slopes to bring to the Irish people a priceless boon, the Faith.

Occasionally on these journeys to "the places where no man dwells" or, as he also writes, "at the ends of the earth," Patrick turned aside to spend whole Lents in solitary prayer and penitential practices. Thus c. 441 he climbed a solitary mountain that raises steep, bare sides 2,510 feet from the shore of Clew Bay, an arm of the Atlantic in present Mayo. Since his day it has been named Croagh Patrick (the Mountain of Patrick). In the solitudes of that lonely peak he communed with God, deepening his own love for his Master and interceding for the Irish children God had given him. He strengthened his soul by enduring in a penitential spirit the fierce gales which the wild North Atlantic storms hurled against his barren mountain. He had but a pitiful structure, raised by his own hands, to protect him from the snow, the rain and the piercing cold. At another time, during a journey to the remote northwest, Patrick spent a Lent praying and fasting on an island in the desolate Lough Derg (of the present Donegal). Although the date cannot be ascertained, an immemorial tradition traces veneration of Lough Derg back to the times of St. Patrick; this tradition has never been contradicted. In subsequent generations the island and the pilgrimage have come to be called the Purgatory of St. Patrick. Today it is one of the three great pilgrimage-places of Ireland.

The work of St. Patrick and his missionaries proceeded steadily onward. Churches had to be built in almost every district in Ireland. One church of especial importance was that which was erected within a few miles of Cruachan, the ancient seat of the kings of Connacht. Patrick named the church Basilica Sanctorum, the Royal Church of the Saints. According to a tradition, tracing back to Patrician days, it was one of the chief episcopal sees of Ireland. Patrick's visit to Cruachan will forever be remembered by his meeting and his conversion of two lovely maidens, Ethna and Fidelmia, the daughters of the High-King Loaghaire. It is the most beautiful story in all the lives of the Irish Saints. Of the south of Ireland, the great kingdom of Munster, there is little of definite detail about St. Patrick's works there. Legends abound, of course, as elsewhere. He is said to have labored in Muskerry and to have visited Cashel. But it is questionable whether the dynasty of Munster had chosen Cashel as its seat during the lifetime of St. Patrick. Professor MacNeill believes that the saint founded a church in the hill country south of Kilmallock (present Tipperary), which was later called Ardpatrick (Patrick's Height). He admits the possiblity that Patrick may have designated this church as the seat of the chief bishop of Munster. Later on, the dignity would have passed to Cashel. Bury, discussing St. Patrick in Munster, says: "If, as is possible, Christianity had made greater way in the southern kingdoms, he had less to do as a pioneer, but the task of organization must have devolved upon him here as in the north."

Continually was the apostle of the Irish ordaining bishops, priests, and deacons; as he says: "God granted me such great grace...that clerics should everywhere be ordained for a people newly come to the faith whom the Lord took from the ends of the earth." Ordaining clerics included for Patrick and his assistants more than liturgical ceremonies. It meant the training of aspirants in holiness, the educating of them in Latin and in sacerdotal studies, the copying by hand of mass-books and psalm-books, the production of altar-breads and altar-wine, and the making of sacred vestments and altar-linens—all preliminary to the priesthood, but all essential.

St. Patrick, a practical man always, concentrated his first efforts on the kings, the ris, the seven great ones, and the hundred and twenty or more minor ones, in the hope that their conversion would lead to their subjects following their example. With some he was unsuccessful, notably the High-King Laoghaire; but from almost all of the kings, including Laoghaire, he obtained permission to preach and convert. The meeting with the High-King Laoghaire at Tara has been embellished with most fantastic and dramatic legends. The meeting was of great importance, for, although the actual power of the High-King was limited to the kingdom of Tara, his prestige as the principal monarch was accepted through the whole of Ireland. Another instance of Patrick's common sense was his organization of dioceses. Heretofore the Church had located dioceses in the principal cities of the Roman Empire and had endowed them with jurisdiction over the surrounding area. But there were no cities in Ireland. The unit was the tuath, or minor kingdom. Patrick created the dioceses in the minor kingdoms and gave to each diocese jurisdiction over the areas that the particular minor kingdom occupied.

Still another example of Patrick's wise judgment was his promotion of a native clergy. Several times he mentions as a special mark of the success of his mission, the ordination of priests and bishops of Irish birth. He did not seem to have great difficulties in finding young men suitable for the priesthood. Possibly in the beginning he chose out young boys, such as Benignus and Sacellus, and kept them constantly in his company, training them in holiness and priestly learning. Such lads were called "pueri Patricii" (Patrick's boys). Many of them became bishops: Benignus, Patrick's successor in Armagh; Sacellus, the bishop of "Basilica Sanctorum" near Cruachan; Fiach, the first native bishop to the Leinstermen; Cathech, the bishop of Bri Garad; and Erc, possibly the bishop of Slane. As the Christians multiplied, candidates for the clerical life had to be recruited on a wider scale. Most likely many were drawn from the local nobility and had been trained in the druidical schools. Ancient biographers seemed to enjoy recounting Patrick's conflicts with the pagan druids and his ultimate complete triumphs; but they could just as well have told of the collaborations of the converted druids, now to be called bards or brehons. Dubhthach, rising to salute St. Patrick at Tara, and St. Fiach, Dubhthach's pupil, are types of such. In the druidical, now bardic, schools the students would have been magnificently trained in habits of study, by the discipline of the memory, and they could have achieved a high culture from familiarity with the old heroic sagas and the poems of the Fianna.

One of St. Patrick's greatest triumphs was his introduction of monastic life among his Irish converts. He marveled at their enthusiasm:

How, then, are the people of Ireland, who never had the knowledge of God, but until now worshiped idols and unclean things, how are they lately been made a people of the Lord, and are called the sons of God? The sons of the Irish and the daughters of their kings are seen to become monks and virgins of Christ.

He cannot restrain his admiration at the numbers: "And the sons of the Scots and the daughters of their chieftains who were monks and virgins of Christ, I am unable to reckon." He writes down an inspiring account of the vocation of a young noble lady; and in the next passage he gives a special word of tribute to the slave-girls, who endure terrors and threats and yet still follow courageously their holy ideals. Scarcely a hundred years elapsed after Patrick's death when Ireland was maintaining so many monasteries as to be given the name, "The Isle of Saints and Scholars." Nothing more clearly proved the solidity of Patrick's apostolate.

The conversion of Ireland was by no means an idyllic pastoral romance. Time and again St. Patrick and his followers had to steel their hearts to the utmost courage to face persecution and obloquy. Patrick summarizes it all: "I shall briefly say in what manner the most gracious God often rescued men from slavery and from the twelve dangers in which my life was imperilled, besides many plots, which I am not able to express in words, lest I should weary my readers." He had to suffer severe criticism from fellow Christians in Gaul, Britain, and Ireland. He wrote his *Confession* to answer their aspersions that he was unlearned and uncultured, that he was incapable in his methods and indiscreet in rushing into situations for which he was sadly unprepared. His *Letter*, in which he excoriated Coroticus for his savage cruelties on Patrick's recently baptized converts, and in which he demanded his excommunication, brought down upon him the enmity of some of his British clerical brethren. They considered Coroticus' raid as a reprisal for former Irish invasions. Patrick had to endure in Ireland charges of self-seeking, of personal ambition, of receiving gifts from converts, and even from some whom he had ordained. He appealed for vindication to his fellow-workers, Auxilius, Iserninus and others of the Auxerre clergy. He made it an iron principle to refuse the gifts of Christian brethren, of virgins and of his converts, who were often gravely disappointed by his refusal. Finally he challenged anyone to show that he had received even a half-scruple (about a shilling), or that he had ever asked from those whom he ordained even the price of a sandal.

But there were far more sinister dangers: the bitter opposition of druids who persisted in their heathenism, the chains of imprisonment and even the proximate threat of death. Patrick notes: "For daily I expect either murder, or robbery, or enslavement." Again he writes down: "Nevertheless they seized me with my companions. And on that day they most eagerly desired to kill me; but my time had not yet come. And everything they found with us they plundered, and myself they bound in chains." But one thing the hero-apostle of the Irish people desired with all his heart: it was to suffer martyrdom for his beloved Master:

> And if ever I accomplish anything good for the sake of my God whom I love, I beg Him to grant me that I may shed my blood with those exiles and captives for His name, even though I should lack burial itself, or my corpse most miserably be torn limb from limb by dogs and wild beasts, or the fowls of the air devour it.

Some years before his death St. Patrick resigned his position as bishop of Armagh, and was succeeded by his disciple St. Benignus. Dr. Bury suggests 457 as a possible date. Patrick would then be about seventy. He spent the last four years of his life at the not too distant Saul, on the southern shore of Strangford Lough, the very place where he began his apostolate. His health was broken by the strain of his austerities and endless journeys. Yet some assert that it was in these years of retirement that Patrick wrote his *Confession;* others, however, assign an earlier date. It is certain that in the last active years as bishop he held a synod at Armagh, from which he and his early companions, Bishop Auxilius and Bishop Iserninus produced the *Collectio Canonum Hibernensium* (the Collection of the Canons of the Irish Church). Following the lead of Tirechan, one of his earliest biographers, some place Patrick's sojourn on Croagh Patrick in this last period of his life. At length St. Patrick, apostle of the people of Ireland, died at Saul, March 17, 461.

Thirty years before he had come to a race that was almost entirely heathen; he left it almost completely Christian, even profoundly so, as the centuries would prove. It was all the work of St. Patrick.

PHOTO BY THE AUTHC

Eamhain Macha (c. 300 B.C.)
The original site of Armagh

The Repositories of St. Patrick's Legacy

The repositories of St. Patrick's legacy for his spiritual sons and daughters are the two documents, his *Confession* and his *Letter to the Soldiers of Coroticus.* Both are genuine and authentic writings; and all modern Patrician scholars accept them as such. The apostle of Ireland composed them in his old age; however there is no need of supposing that this means a time just shortly before his death. Père Grosjean and Doctor Bieler hold as quite certain that the *Letter* was written before the *Confession.*

The cause of the *Letter* was Patrick's indignation at a savage raid into Ireland by Coroticus, a British ruler, one of those native Christian leaders who had stepped into the places of the departed Roman legions. A number of Patrick's newly baptized converts were slaughtered; and many others were enslaved and sold to heathen Scots and Picts. St. Patrick in his epistle excoriated the ruler, demanding his excommunication, and severely castigating those who would still associate with him.

The British clergy became highly incensed with Patrick's letter. They considered Coroticus their champion against Irish raiders, from whom in the past they had suffered grievously. Their angry memories blinded them to the atrocities which Coroticus and his raiders had inflicted on their new fellow-Christians across the Irish Sea. There was a recrudescence of the old objections against Patrick, which years before had been urged to prevent his consecration as bishop of the mission to Ireland. Again there were being circulated those old animadversions: his educational deficiency, his imprudence, his rusticity, his lack of culture, his want of experience. And to them were added complaints from Irish enemies: charges of self-interest and simony, and (probably from hostile druids) the reproach of being a foreign intruder. Such ill repute, spreading through Britain, Gaul, and even Ireland, could spell complete disaster for Patrick's Irish apostolate.

To prevent this catastrophe St. Patrick wrote his *Confession*. The work is essentially a spiritual document. Patrick's method of vindicating his apostolate was to reveal the workings of

God's grace in his missionary soul.[1] "Confession" here has the meaning of a witnessing before men of God's goodness and God's graces. St. Matthew, 10:32, has it: "Everyone therefore that shall confess Me before men, I will confess him before My Father who is in Heaven." St. Paul in his *Second Epistle to the Corinthians* made just such a confession. Patrick was familiar with St. Paul's work and borrowed much from it. However Patrick's *Confession* is not without some elements of St. Augustine's idea—the contrite accounting of evil transgressions. St. Patrick frankly admitted the sins of his youth and humbly avowed his human weaknesses. But the transgressions of his early years were minor incidents of his life-story. What were now being asserted against him were supposed deficiencies as a bishop and alleged shortcomings as a missionary.

St. Patrick's apologia was not cast in formal lines—listing of charges and refutations of them in detail. His way was: first to establish that God had chosen him to be the bishop of the Irish nation, then to make known the graces which God had bestowed upon him for the task, and finally to show how he responded to these divine favors. Everything was from God or for God with St. Patrick. Few saints have been more absorbingly dedicated to the Divinity; few have been more intensely grateful to God.

---

[1]This method of vindication St. Patrick also put into his *Letter to the Soldiers of Coroticus.*

And so in the measure of our faith in the Trinity it is fitting for me to explain and without censure of rashness to make known the gift of God and the everlasting hope. Moreover it is fitting that I spread everywhere the name of God without fear, confidently; so that after my death I may leave a legacy to my brethren and my sons whom I baptized in the Lord—so many thousands of men.

(*Confession*, 14)

It may well be conjectured that even if St. Patrick had not to compose a vindication, he still would have written the *Confession* as a memorial of his mission, his ideals and his deeds, verily a legacy for his children.

To St. Patrick the most vital fact was God's choice of him to be Bishop of the Irish nation. Patrick was the only bishop in the first seven years of the mission; and he was the supreme prelate in the hierarchy of the later-organized church. He was insistent on his unique bishopric in both of his writings. "I avow that I have been established a bishop in Ireland. Most assuredly I believe that I have received from God what I am." (*Letter*, 1.) He concluded his account of the vision in which he had heard the cry of the Irish, "We beseech thee, holy youth, to come and walk once more amongst us," with these words: "Thanks to God, after many years the Lord granted to them according to their earnest cry." (*Confession*, 23.) The earlier campaign against Patrick revolved about one proposal, that he be made the bishop in the new Irish mission. On the night following his rejection Patrick received a vision in which he beheld a writing void of honor opposite his face, and heard the voice of God saying to him, "We have seen with pain the fact of the (bishop) designate stripped of his due title." (*Confession*, 29.) Patrick, describing his missionary labors in remote parts of Ireland, depicted himself ordaining clerics, administering confirmation and organizing dioceses. These were all episcopal functions; and St. Patrick was exercising them as the supreme bishop of Ireland.

The second and third elements of his apologia, the heavenly graces bestowed and his responses to them, St. Patrick treated in combinations of a particular grace and the respondent virtue. The treatments were numerous and are scattered through both writings. The present chapter will leave to the reader the seeking out of the graces and the responses. Personal discovery will prove most rewarding. First there will be the encountering of Patrick the saint just as an old Irish panegyrist of a thousand years ago styled him: "a just man with purity of nature ...gentle, forgiving of heart...a man full of grace and of the knowledge of the Holy Spirit...a fair garden of virtues...a bright fire of fervor... and burning charity...a laborious and serviceable slave of Christ."[1] Secondly there will be the comprehending to the full of St. Patrick's legacy, which is the exemplification of his ideals and virtues in God's cause. To assist recurrent and reflective studying of the legacy there has been

[1]Quoted by Francis Shaw, S.J., in his admirable study, *The Real St. Patrick*, Dublin, 1931.

placed, after the text of the two writings, an appendix which lists the saint's principal virtues and also the numbers of the paragraphs in the *Confession* and in the *Letter* where particular virtues appear.

What of Patrick's abilities and methods as a writer? A cursory perusal of his two authentic works might leave a casual reader with the impression of a mixed jumble of factual data, personal opinions, biblical quotations and prayerful supplications—the digressive reminiscences of an old man. A more thoughtful reading, with Patrick's purposes and life-experiences steadily kept in mind, would produce a much higher evaluation, and a truer one. The Bollandist, Père Paul Grosjean, a formidable critic indeed, declared that St. Patrick left in his *Confession* "one of the most moving relics of Latin, nay more of Christian, literature."

St. Patrick, as he himself so often admitted, was not a scholar. How could he have been, with his heedless boyhood, his slave days in Ireland, and his monastic years—concerned primarily with prayer and penitence, and only after these, with a working knowledge of the Scriptures and a basic theology? Neither was Patrick a man of letters. He says very honestly: "From the savor of my writings it can easily be perceived how little I have been instructed and trained in languages." *(Confession,* 9.) The patriarch of the Irish, occupied with a hundred tasks, wrote only when forced by the urgencies of his episcopal office or the defense of his

Irish apostolate. His total literary remains are: the two writings, the *Confession* and the *Letter;* a few sentences from lost letters; and a brief collection of canons (rules) for ecclesiastical discipline, issued conjointly by the bishops, Patrick, Auxilius, and Iserninus—though probably composed largely by Patrick.

Two ancient documents connected with St. Patrick should be mentioned here. One is the *Hymn in Patrick's Praise.* It is a Latin work, written during the lifetime of the saint by one of his first assistant bishops, St. Secundinus. The hymn gives a very factual portrayal of the patriarch working in his Irish apostolate. Père Grosjean suggests, with great probability, that Secundinus wrote his verses to defend his superior against the charges of the critics who were aroused by Patrick's condemnation of Coroticus. The second document is the *Lorica,* or *Breastplate of St. Patrick.* Written in Gaelic, it was long attributed to St. Patrick. It is a morning prayer, and an invocation of the Holy Trinity. Its present form dates from about the ninth century; but much of its structure and very many of its expressions indicate a far earlier composing. Dr. Bieler says that its origin with St. Patrick is a possibility that should not be rashly dismissed.[1] At least the assertion could be made that it was in the fashion of the *Lorica* that St. Patrick might often have prayed.

---

[1]Ludwig Bieler, Ph.D. *The Works of St. Patrick,* Westminster, Md. U.S.A.; London, 1953.

Patrick's literary capabilities can be judged, of course, only from his two completed works, and especially from the *Confession* which is thrice the length of the *Letter* and covers a far wider range of ideas. Though the saint had no intention of writing an autobiography, he did put a good deal of biographical data into the *Confession,* and even some into the *Letter.* The two documents are the main sources, and the only authentic ones, for the greater part of his life-story.

Yet it is in the historical elements that Patrick's writings suffer the most. A coherent narrative exists only in the *Confession,* paragraphs 1 and 2, which tell of his birth and boyhood, and paragraphs 16 to 23, which describe his years of slavery in Ireland, his escape to Gaul, and his eventual return to his family in Britain. Even in these paragraphs Patrick seems to be interested only in what is spiritually significant. For instance, he makes no mention here of an important fact about the boat in which he escaped from Ireland, that its cargo was Irish wolfhounds. Only later does he make a casual allusion to this fact, during his description of the subsequent journey through a deserted area and the starvation that befell himself, the crew, and their cargo of hounds. Elsewhere in his writings when Patrick introduces biographical data, he does so only to illustrate a point of spirituality, without any consideration for chronology. This deficiency is particularly notable in the account of his rejection and rehabilitation. It is also present in the discussions of his missionary work. In the latter accounts he writes little that is definite about his missionary methods, or about his achievements in organizing churches and dioceses. For a fuller knowledge some help may be found in the *Canons of Patrick, Auxilius, and Iserninus,* in St. Secundinus' *Hymn,* and in the traditions of the Patrician churches collected by Tirechan.

The writings of St. Patrick disclose little about his ecclesiastical practice and knowledge. They reveal next to nothing about the liturgy which he used. They give something more about his dogmatic positions, especially his teaching on the Catholic doctrine of grace. The source of this last was the training which he received at Auxerre under St. Germanus; in fact Patrick's Irish mission grew out of this great orthodox prelate's own mission against the Pelagian heretics in Britain. But one fact the writings certainly do manifest, Patrick's extraordinary familiarity with the Holy Scriptures. The *Confession* and the *Letter,* printed together, cover only about twenty-eight printed pages, yet they have embodied in their texts no fewer than 190 quotations or citations from Holy Writ.

When instancing historical deficiencies in the *Confession* and in the *Letter* one should keep in mind that Patrick had no intention of writing these documents as his own complete biography. Rather, first and immediately, he was composing a defense of his Irish apostolate;

then, secondly and, more farsightedly, he was producing a legacy of spirituality for his flock and their descendants. In the writing of his defense Patrick took for granted in his readers, disciples or critics, a general knowledge of the facts and incidents of the conflict; hence he considered it unnecessary to be more fully detailed or explicit. The time which had elapsed was brief, scarcely more than two decades. The areas concerned were not large, not numerously populated; Auxerre and the country round about it in northern Gaul, the southern half of Britain, and mostly in its western sections, and Ireland.

It may appear strange to a modern reader that Patrick treated the second conference on his Irish apostolate first. To himself and his contemporaries the second conference was far more important than the first conference wherein hardly more than Patrick's name was mentioned. It was in the second that the powerful opposition arose against him and succeeded in bringing about his rejection, especially after the proposal to make him a bishop. And now, once more, these old objections were being heard against him. The answering of them was the reason why Patrick composed the apologia of his *Confession.* An example of Patrick's inaccuracy occurs in this connection when he says: "And when I was attacked by certain of my elders, who came and urged my sins against my laborious episcopate." *(Confession,* 26.) A footnote in the text explains: "The words 'laborious episcopate' were made by the saint in retrospect." A weary old bishop may be pardoned for placing his missionary work before the previous attacks that had been made to prevent its coming into existence. There can be no doubt that St. Patrick presupposed a general knowledge both of his reinstatement in the mission to Ireland and of his later accomplishments during his Irish apostolate; for he could write: "and my faith has been approved before God and men." (*Confession*, 30.) Patrick's composing the *Confession* and the *Letter* in his old age may explain somewhat the defects of cohesion and of logical order. He must have had to rely much upon his memories for it is hardly possible that he possessed any considerable collection of written records. As he wrote, or very probably dictated, he gave to the ideas that came crowding in upon him the place and importance that he deemed them to deserve.

The *Confession*, on its first reading, may prove somewhat confusing. To help for a clearer comprehension the following sketchy outline of contents is offered: Biographical facts of boyhood, 1; Reasons for writing and difficulties of the task, 2 - 15; Captivity and escape, 16 - 23; Vocation, 23 - 25; Opposition, 26 - 33; Gratitude to God for vocation, protection and favors, 34 - 36; Devotion to apostolate, 37; Missionary work (in general), 37 - 43; God's grace for the mission and Patrick's grateful responses, 43 - 51; Mission methods, desire for martyrdom, 52 - 59; Adoration of the Holy Trinity, 60; Patrick's prinicipal motivation in his apostolate, 61; Conclusion - reference of all to God, 62.

The *Letter to the Soldiers of Coroticus* is easier to comprehend. It is much briefer, less than a third the length of the *Confession.* It has one central theme, a fiery protest against the outrageous crimes of murdering or selling into slavery the newly-baptized Irish Christians. It is better organized: Patrick's insistence on his authority as apostolic bishop of the Irish to write for them; his excoriation of the atrocious deeds and of their perpetrators; his warning to clerics against associating with these criminals; his expression of his personal anguish for the unfortunate victims; his final denunciation of the merciless evildoers; his appeal to God, the apostles, and the prophets; his concluding wish for repentance of Coroticus and his soldiers.

St. Patrick's style in the *Confession* and in the *Letter* is uniquely personal. His Latin was not that of the writer, but of the orator. Yet it was not of the Roman orator, whose polished discourses are world classics, but of the popular preacher—improvised, prompted on the spur of the emotion and the moment. Père Grosjean declared St. Patrick was a born preacher, whose words in the two documents were direct, manly, strong, and powerful, and went straight into the souls of his hearers. If the listeners were recent converts, and still more if they were yet pagans, Patrick, the missionary, in explaining the truths of faith and in exhorting to Christian morals, was especially put to holding their attention. Frequently he had to declaim intensely and emotionally: pausing dramatically, interrupting abruptly his discoursing, uttering rapid asides, developing longer parentheses, stressing heavily vital points, appealing to the living and apostrophizing the absent or the dead. This is all vivid, soul-stirring preaching; and it is the distinctive style of Patrick's two documents. But it is not the Latin of the fifth century senator or pedagogue. Patrick, it is worth recalling, was writing, especially in the *Confession*, an important letter (on which hung all the prospects of his Irish Mission) to cultured clerics, citizens of the Roman Empire, "who in the most approved fashion have drunk in both law and Holy Scripture alike, and who never changed from infancy their mother tongue, but rather have been always rendering it more perfect." *(Confession,* 9.) No wonder a note of diffidence appears from time to time in Patrick's writings.

A disconnectedness, a sort of staccato emphasis, also marks Patrick's style. It comes from his use of interpreters during the early years of his apostolate. "My words and discourses are translated into a tongue foreign to me." *(Confession,* 9.) Originally Patrick spoke Latin. It was the language of his boyhood and also of the more than twenty years he later spent in Gaul. Patrick also spoke Irish. He acquired it in the six years of his slavery, and of course he used it continually during his ministry. Did he ever master the language of the Gaels completely? Certainly in the early years in Erin he could not have become a fluent speaker of *cultured* Irish. Perhaps he never did achieve that proficiency. Like the Homeric Greeks, the ancient Irish had produced an oral literature; and like that of the patriarchal Greeks, theirs had not been written down until centuries after its composition. The rich poetry of the Red Branch Cycle and of the Fenian Cycle were not inscribed on manuscripts until after the death of St. Patrick.[1] The custodians of this spoken literature were the *filidh*, the class of professional poets. Those among them who would furnish a foreigner with a wide knowledge of Irish could effect little, because they lacked the written vocabularies and grammars which he would need. The *filidh* gained their own felicity with words in the long years of memory-training which they had to submit to in their youth. Obviously, a middle-aged bishop, burdened with the tasks of establishing a missionary church, had neither the time nor the capabilities for such a regimen.

St. Patrick turned to the interpreters. Their employment was normal procedure in the early Church. But the constant use of interpreters could ruin the polished art of any Roman orator. Paragraphs and long sentences were cut up. Each small section was translated and delivered to the assembled gathering in the presence of of the preacher. And so bit by bit the whole

[1] Script writing was brought to the Irish language by St. Patrick or by some contemporaries of his.

sermon was gotten through. But during the process usually there were frequent interruptions, additions, and corrections, for the interpreter might have misunderstood, or deviated from the original. Always the preacher had to measure his thoughts and words to the capabilities of his listeners—or even of his interpreter. How difficult it must have been finding Irish words to express the profound and exact thoughts of the Greco-Roman theologians of the fifth century! This halting preaching through interpreters over so many years, along with the endless struggle against misunderstanding, forced Patrick into a habit of discontinuity in his writings—or rather dictations.

Structure and style are after all of secondary importance in the study of St. Patrick's legacy. The knowledge of his virtues and the revelations of his zeal are the primary concerns. These are what the patriarch wished his children and his clients to cherish and to make their own. His legacy can be possessed first by a reverent reading of the texts of the *Confession* and of the *Letter,* and then by meditative rereadings.

And so, as Father Shaw, S.J., so well concludes his study, *The Real St. Patrick:*[1]

> By becoming familiar with the *Confession,* we shall secure certainly that Patrick will "come again and walk once more amongst us," for here in his own writings, shall we find the real Patrick an intensely lovable character, a man human

[1] Rev. Francis Shaw, S.J., *The Real St. Patrick,* Irish Messenger, Dublin, 1931.

like ourselves, grieved by the treachery of a friend, longing for the companionship of home and brethren, hurt by the sneers of critics, yet a man truly Christlike in spirit, meek and humble, simple and straightforward, practicing Evangelical poverty, a man filled with an ardent personal love for Christ and burning with zeal for the salvation of souls, trusting in God for all things, desiring with great desire to die for Christ, in natural character a man energetic, resolute, indomitable, and possessed of an exceptional talent for organization and for government. Such a one was Patrick, the missioner whom God elected in those days out of all the world to bring "tidings of great joy" to those "men of good will" "who dwelt by the Western sea."

St. Patrick's Bell

This little cow-bell, of iron dipped in bronze, is the oldest instrument of its kind in Ireland; it was made about 406. In the third edition of Wakeman-Cooke's *Handbook of Irish Antiquities*, on page 346, may be read: "There is good reason to believe that, as its name implies, it had belonged to St. Patrick himself." This view was held by Father Herbert Thurston S.J., the strictest of critics. For many ages it was treasured at Armagh. It is now displayed at the National Museum, Dublin.

In our own day this venerable bell was heard once again. It was at the Consecration during the Solemn Mass concluding the World Eucharistic Congress of 1932, held at Dublin to commemorate the Fifteenth Centenary of St. Patrick's Irish Apostolate. In the mighty silence that rested on the enormous crowd in vast Phoenix Park, high up on the great altar, the celebrant had completed the sacred words. Then the presence of the Eucharistic God was proclaimed to the silent throng, not by flourishes of silver trumpets, nor by the crash of artillery-salutes. No, but by the ringing of St. Patrick's Bell. Its gentle pealings, carried by modern communication, were telling Ireland and all Ireland's friends in the whole world that Jesus, their God-King had come. Fifteen hundred years ago St. Patrick had rung that same bell to tell them that the Divine Savior had come to the people of Erin.

The Shrine of St. Patrick's Bell. 1091-1105

Brass, with ornaments of silver-gilt, gold and precious gems. It is the finest of the bell-shrines.

Front (left), Reverse (right).

On exhibition at the National Museum. Dublin.

THE LEGACY OF SAINT PATRICK

Confession of St. Patrick

1. I, Patrick, the sinner, am the most rustic and the least of all the faithful, and contemptible in the eyes of very many. I had for my father Calpornius, a deacon, a son of Potitus, a priest, who belonged to the village of Bannavem Taberniae. Now he had a small villa hard by, where I was taken captive.

At that time I was barely sixteen years of age. I knew not the true God;[1] and I was led into captivity in Ireland with many thousands of persons, in accordance with our deserts, for we turned away from God, and kept not His com-

[1]Patrick was a heedless Christian youth, not a pagan.

mandments, and were not obedient to our priests, who were wont to admonish us for our salvation. And the Lord brought upon us the indignation of His wrath, and scattered us among many nations even to the ends of the earth, where now my littleness may be seen amongst strangers.

2. And there the Lord opened up the understanding of my unbelief so that at length I might recall to my mind my sins, and that I might be converted with all my heart to the Lord my God, who hath regarded my humility, and taken pity on my youth and my ignorance, and kept watch over me before I knew Him, and before I had discernment or could distinguish between good and evil, and protected and consoled me as a father does his son.

3. Wherefore, I cannot keep silence—nor would it be fitting—concerning such great benefits and such great grace as the Lord has vouchsafed to bestow on me in the land of my captivity; for this is the return we make, that after our chastening or after our recognition of God, we should exalt and proclaim His wondrous ways before every nation which is under the whole heaven.

4. Because there is no other God, nor has there been heretofore, nor will there be hereafter, except God the Father unbegotten, without beginning, from whom is all beginning, upholding all things, as we say, and His Son Jesus Christ, whom we likewise confess to have always been with the Father—before the world's beginning spiritually and ineffably of the Father begotten before all beginning; and by Him were made all things visible and invisible. He was made man, and, having triumphed over death, was taken up to the Father in heaven. And He (the Father) gave to Him all power above every name, so that at the name of Jesus every knee should bend of those that are in heaven, on earth, and under the earth, and every tongue should confess to Him that Jesus Christ is the Lord and God in whom we believe, and whose coming we expect will soon take place, the Judge of the living and the dead, who will render to everyone according to his works; and who hath poured out on us abundantly the Holy Ghost, the gift and pledge of our immortality, who maketh those who believe and obey become sons of God and joint heirs with Christ, whom we confess and adore as one God in the Trinity of the Sacred Name.

5. For He Himself through the prophet saith: "Call upon me in the day of trouble and I will deliver thee; and thou shalt glorify Me." And again He saith: "It is honorable to reveal and confess the works of God."

6. Yet, although I am faulty in many things, I wish my brethren and kinfolk to know what

manner of man I am, so that they may be able to understand the desire of my soul.

7. I am not ignorant of the testimony of my Lord, who witnesseth in the psalm: "Thou wilt destroy those who speak a lie." And again He saith: "The idle word that men shall speak they shall render an account for it in the day of judgment."

8. Therefore I ought to dread exceedingly, with fear and trembling, this sentence on that day when no one will be able to absent himself or hide, but when all of us—every one—shall have to give an account of his smallest sins before the judgment seat of Christ the Lord.

9. For this reason I have long since thought of writing, but I hesitated up till now; for I feared lest I should fall under the censure of men's tongues, seeing that I am not learned like others, who in the most approved fashion have drunk in both law and Holy Scripture alike, and who have never changed from infancy their mother tongue, but rather have been always rendering it more perfect.

My words and discourses are translated into a tongue foreign to me. From the savor of my writings it can easily be perceived how little I have been instructed and trained in languages; for, as the Wise Man saith: "By the tongue wisdom will be discerned, and understanding, and knowledge, and learning of the truth."

10. But what availeth an excuse, though in accordance with truth, especially if it is combined with presumption? As if, forsooth, now in my old age I were to covet that which in my youth I did not acquire, because my sins prevented me from mastering what I had barely read through earlier in life. But who gives me credence even when I repeat what I have said at the outset?

When a mere youth, nay a beardless boy, I was taken captive before I knew what I ought to seek, or what I ought to avoid. And therefore even today I am ashamed and dread exceedingly to lay bare my inexperience. Because, not being learned, I cannot explain my meaning in a few words; for as the Spirit desireth, both mind and sense disclose their affections.

11. Yet even had I that gift of speech like others, still I would not keep silence on account of the reward. And if perchance it seems to many that I am thrusting myself forward in this matter with my want of knowledge and my slower tongue, yet it is written: "The stammering tongue shall quickly learn to speak peace." How much more should I long to do this who am, as the apostle saith, the epistle of Christ for salvation unto the ends of the earth, and, although not an eloquent one, still a most powerful decree written in your hearts, not with ink, but with the Spirit of the Living God. And again the

Spirit witnesseth: "Rusticity, too, was ordained by the Most High."

12. Whence I, who was at first a rustic, an exile, unlearned surely as one who knows not how to provide for the future—but this I do most certainly know, that before I was humbled I was like a stone lying in the deep mire, and He that is mighty came, and in His mercy lifted me up and indeed raised me aloft, and placed me on the top of the wall. And therefore I ought to cry aloud so that I may render something to the Lord for His benefits which are so great both here and for eternity, that the mind of man cannot estimate them.

13. Wherefore then be ye filled with wonder, ye great and little who fear God, and ye too, lordly rhetoricians, hear and ponder over this. Who was it that exalted me, fool though I be, from the midst of those who seem to be wise and skilled in the law, and powerful in word and in everything else? And me, truly despicable in this world, He inspired beyond others—if such I were—that with fear and reverence and without blame I should faithfully serve the nation to whom the love of Christ transferred and bestowed me for the duration of my life, if I should be worthy; in a word that I should with humility and truth serve them.

14. And so in the measure of our faith in the Trinity it is fitting for me to explain and without censure of rashness to make known the gift of God and the everlasting hope. Moreover it is fitting that I spread everywhere the name of God without fear, confidently; so that after my death I may leave a legacy to my brethren and my sons whom I baptized in the Lord—so many thousands of men.

15. And I was not worthy, nor was I such that the Lord should grant this to His poor servant after calamities and such great difficulties, after a life of slavery, after so many years; that He should bestow on me this great grace in favor of that nation—something that formerly, in my youth, I never hoped nor prayed for.

16. Now after I came to Ireland, daily I herded flocks; and often during the day I prayed. The love of God and the fear of Him increased more and more, and my faith grew, and my spirit was stirred up, so that in a single day I said as many as a hundred prayers, and at night nearly as many, even while I was out in the woods and on the mountain. Before dawn I used to arouse myself to prayer in snow and frost and rain; and I minded no pain, nor was there any sluggishness in me, as I now feel, because then the spirit was fervent within me.

17. And there truly one night I heard in my sleep a voice saying to me: "Thou fastest well; soon thou wilt go to thy fatherland." And, again, after a very short time I heard the heavenly voice saying to me: "Lo, thy ship is ready." And it was not near at hand, but was distant, perhaps, two hundred miles. And I had never been there, nor did I know any person living there. And thereupon I shortly took to flight, and left the man with whom I had been for six years. And I came in the strength of God who prospered my way for good; and I met with nothing to alarm me until I reached that ship.

18. And on the very day that I arrived, the ship was pulled down from the shore; and I said that I had the wherewith to sail thence with them. But my request displeased the captain, and with anger he replied harshly, "On no account seek thou to go with us."

When I heard this I left them, to go to the hut where I was lodging. On the way I began to pray; and before I finished my prayer I heard one of them shouting loudly after me: "Come quickly, for these men are calling thee." And straightway I returned to them.

And they began to say to me: "Come, we take thee in good faith; make friendship with us in any way thou desirest." And so on that day I refused to suck their breasts,[1] through

---

[1]A symbolic expression used by heathens in Pre-Christian Ireland when appealing for formal protection and intimate friendship; similarly, "grasping of the cheeks," or "seizing of the knees." St. Patrick did not wish close intimacy with the pagans.

the fear of God. But nevertheless I hoped that some of them would come into the faith of Christ, for they were heathens; and on this account I stayed with them. And forthwith we set sail.

19. And after three days we made land, and we journeyed for twenty-eight days through deserted country. Food failed them, and hunger overtook them. And one day the captain began to say to me: "What sayest thou, Christian? Thy God is great and almighty, why then canst thou not pray for us? For we are in grave danger of starvation; it is hardly probable that we shall ever see a human being again." Then I said plainly to them: "Turn earnestly and with all your hearts to the Lord my God, to whom nothing is impossible, that this day He may send you food in your journey until you be satisfied, for He has abundance everywhere."

And, by the help of God, so it came to pass. Lo, a herd of swine appeared on the road before our eyes. The crew killed many of them; and in that place they spent two nights; and they were well refreshed. Their hounds also were sated, for many of them had become weak from hunger, and were left half-dead by the way.

And after this the men gave greatest thanks to God, and I became honored in their eyes. From that day they had food in abundance. They also found wild honey and offered me a part.

But one of them said, "This is an idol-offering." Thanks be to God, I tasted none of it thereafter.

20. Now on that same night when I was sleeping, Satan tempted me mightily, in such sort as I shall remember as long as I am in this body. And there fell upon me, as it were, a huge rock, and I had no power over my limbs. But whence did it come into my mind, I know not, to invoke Helias? And thereupon I saw the sun rise in the heaven, and whilst I kept shouting "Helias, Helias," with all my might, lo, the splendor of that sun fell upon me, and straightway shook all weight from off me.[1] And I believe that I was aided by Christ my Lord, and that His Spirit was even then calling aloud on my behalf. And I hope that it will be so in the day of my distress; as He saith in the Gospel: "In that day," the Lord witnesseth, "it is not you that speak, but the Spirit of your Father that speaketh in you."

21. And again, after many years more, I was taken captive. And so on that first night I

---

[1]Dr. Bieler, the noted Patrician scholar, explains this incident by suggesting a fusion in St. Patrick's mind of the prophet Elias and the sun god Helios. This fusion, common in early Christian art, arose from (a) the similarity of the names in Greek, and (b) the parallel of the assumption of the prophet in a fiery chariot into heaven and the pagan legend of the sun god driving his chariot through the sky. Dr. Bieler also declares that St. Patrick understood the sun that dispelled his temptation to be Christ, the true Sun of salvation.

emained with them. Moreover I heard a divine oice saying to me: "For two months more thou vilt be with them." And so it came to pass, on he sixtieth night thereafter, the Lord delivered ne out of their hands.

22. Moreover He provided for us food and ire and dry quarters every day until on the tenth lay we all reached our destination. As I stated efore, for twenty-eight days we journeyed hrough deserted country. And on the night on which we all reached our destination, we had n truth no food left.

23. And once more, after a few years, I was n Britain with my family. They received me as a son and earnestly besought me that now at least, after so many tribulations which I had undergone, I should never depart from them.

And there indeed I saw in a vision of the night a man whose name was Victoricus coming as it were from Ireland with countless letters. He gave me one of them, and I read the beginning of the letter, which was entitled, "The Voice of the Irish." And whilst I was reading aloud the beginning of the letter I thought that at that very moment I heard the voices of those who dwelt beside the Wood of Foclut, which is nigh unto the Western Sea. And thus they cried, as with one mouth, "We beseech thee, holy youth, to come and walk once more amongst us."

And I was exceedingly touched in my heart and could read no more, and so I awoke. Thanks be to God, after many years the Lord granted to them according to their earnest cry.

24. And on another night, whether within me or beside me, I cannot tell, God knoweth, in most admirable words, which I heard and could not understand, except that at the end of the prayer, He spoke out thus: "He who laid down His life for thee, He it is who speaketh in thee." And so I awoke rejoicing.

25. And another time I saw Him praying in me, and He was as it were within my body; and I heard Him over me, that is over the interior man, and there He was praying mightily with groanings. And meanwhile I was astonished, and was marveling and considering who it could be who was praying within me. But at the end of the prayer He spoke out to the effect that He was the Spirit. And so I awoke, and I remembered the Apostle saying: "The Spirit helpeth the infirmities of our prayer. For we know not what we should pray for as we ought; but the Spirit Himself asketh for us with unspeakable groanings, which cannot be expressed in words." And again: "The Lord our advocate maketh intercession for us."

26. And when I was attacked by certain of my elders, who came and urged my sins against my laborious episcopate,[1] truly on that day I was so cast down that I might have fallen here and in eternity. But the Lord graciously had pity on the stranger and sojourner for His Name's sake, and He helped me exceedingly in that humiliation, so that I did not fall badly into disgrace and reproach. I pray God that the occasion be not reckoned to them as a sin.

27. After the lapse of thirty years they found a cause against me, and it was the word of a confession which I had made before I became a deacon.[2] On account of my anxiety, with sorrowful mind I revealed to my dearest friend what I had done one day in my youth, nay, in one hour, because I was not yet strong. I cannot tell, God knoweth it, if I was then fifteen years old, and I did not believe in the living God, nor had I from my infancy; but I remained in death and unbelief until I had been chastened exceed-

---

[1] Sections 26-33 almost certainly refer to the attempt at preventing Patrick being made a bishop, and not to criticism of his Missionary methods. The words "laborious episcopate" were made by the saint in retrospect. The criticisms were made later during St. Patrick's apostolate.

[2] St. Patrick, when about to become a deacon, in order to quiet his own scruples, confided the sin which he had committed about the age of fifteen to a friend. The friend, fifteen years afterwards, alleged that sin against Patrick's promotion to the episcopate. At that period the age for receiving the diaconate was thirty. So Patrick when he was consecrated bishop must have been about forty-five years of age. There is no question here of sacramental confession; it was counsel which Patrick sought in confidence—"insinuavi amicissimo meo" (I revealed to my dearest friend).

ingly, and humbled in truth by hunger and nakedness, and that daily.

28. However, I did not proceed to Ireland of my own accord until I was nearly worn out. But this was rather well for me, because in this way I was corrected by the Lord. And He prepared me, so that today I am what once was far from me, that I should care for and labor for the salvation of others, whereas at that time I did not even think about myself.

29. On that day, then, on which I was rejected by the persons whom I have mentioned above, during that night I had a vision of the night. There was a writing void of honor opposite my face. And meanwhile I heard the voice of God saying to me: "We have seen with pain the face of the (bishop) designate stripped of his due title." He did not say, "Thou hast seen with pain," but, "We have seen with pain," as if in that matter He had joined Himself with me, as He hath said: "He that toucheth you is as he that toucheth the apple of Mine eye."

30. Therefore I give thanks to Him, who hath strengthened me in all things, so as not to hinder me from the journey on which I had resolved, and from my labor which I had learnt from Christ my Lord. Nay, rather I felt in me no small virtue coming from Him. And my faith has been approved before God and men.[1]

[1] By the success of his mission in Ireland.

31. Wherefore then I say boldly my conscience does not blame me here or hereafter. God is my witness that I have not lied in the statements I have made to you.

32. But rather do I grieve for my dearest friend that we should have deserved to hear such a voice from God as that. To him I had revealed my very soul! And I ascertained from some of the brethren before that investigation—for I myself was not present, nor was I in Britain, nor was it at my request—that he would fight for me in my absence. Even he himself had said to me with his own lips: "Lo, thou art to be raised to the rank of bishop"; of which I was not worthy. But how then did it occur to him afterwards to put me to shame publicly before everyone, good and bad, in respect to that office which before of his own accord and gladly he had conceded to me—and the Lord, too, did, who is greater than all?

33. I have said enough. But nevertheless I ought not to hide the gift of God which He bestowed upon me in the land of my captivity; because then I earnestly sought Him, and there I found Him, and He preserved me from all iniquities. This is my belief, because of His indwelling Spirit who hath worked in me until this day. Boldly again (I am speaking). But God knoweth if man had said this to me, perchance I would have held my peace for the love of Christ.

34. Hence therefore I render unwearied thanks to my God who kept me faithful in the day of my temptation, so that today I can confidently offer to Him a sacrifice, as a living victim, my soul to Christ my Lord, who hath saved me from all my troubles. So I can say: "Who am I, O Lord, or what is my vocation, that Thou hast manifested to me such divine power, so that today I should steadfastly exalt and magnify Thy name among the heathens wherever I may be; and that not only in prosperity but also in afflictions?" So whatever befalls me, whether good or bad, I ought to receive with equal mind, and always give thanks to God who showed me that I might trust Him endlessly, as one that cannot be doubted; and who hath heard me, so that I, ignorant as I am, should in the last days, begin to undertake this work so holy and so wonderful—so that I might imitate, in some degree, those whom the Lord long ago foretold would proclaim His Gospel for a testimony unto all nations before the end of the world. And accordingly, as we see, this too has been fulfilled. Behold, we are witnesses that the Gospel has been preached unto the places beyond which no man dwells.

35. Now, it would be a tedious task to narrate the whole of my toil in all its details, or even partially. I shall briefly say in what manner the most gracious God often rescued me from slavery and from the twelve dangers in which my life was imperiled, besides many plots, which I am not able to express in words, lest I should weary my readers. But I have for my surety God who knoweth all things even before they come to pass, as His divine voice frequently admonished me, poor, humble and unlearned (as I am).

36. Whence came to me this wisdom, which was not in me, I who neither knew the number of my days, nor savored God? Whence afterwards came to me that gift, so great and so salutary, to know God and to love Him, but only that I might part with fatherland and parents?

37. And many gifts were offered to me with weeping and tears. And I displeased the donors, and also, against my wish, some of my seniors; but, God being my guide, I did not at all consent or acquiesce (in their desires). It was not my grace, but God who conquered in me, and He withstood them all, so that I came to the Irish tribes to preach the Gospel, and to endure insults from the unbelievers, so as to hear the reproach of my going abroad, and to suffer many persecutions even unto bonds, and to give up my free condition for the profit of others. And if I should be worthy I am ready to give even my life for His name's sake unhesitatingly and very gladly; and it is there (Ireland) that I desire to spend it until I die, if the Lord would grant it to me.

38. Because I am immensely a debtor t God, who granted me such great grace that man peoples through me should be regenerated unt God and afterwards confirmed, and that cleric should everywhere be ordained for them, for people newly come to the faith, whom the Lor took from the ends of the earth. As He had i times past promised through His prophets: "T thee the Gentiles shall come from the ends o the earth, and shall say: As our fathers have go for themselves false idols, and there is no profi in them." And again: "I have set thee to be th light of the Gentiles, that thou mayest be m salvation to the utmost parts of the earth."

39. And there I wish to await His promis who verily never disappoints; as He promise in the Gospel: "They shall come from the eas and the west, and from the south and from the north, and shall sit down with Abraham and Isaa and Jacob"; as we believe that the faithful wil come from all parts of the world.

40. For that reason, therefore, we ought t fish well and diligently, as the Lord forewarn and teaches: "Come after me and I will make you to be fishers of men." And again He sait through the prophets: "Behold, I send man fishers and hunters," and so forth.

Wherefore, then, it is very necessary that we should spread our nets, so that a great multitude and a throng should be taken for God, and tha everywhere there should be clergy who should baptize and should exhort the poor and the needy people, as the Lord in the Gospel warns and teaches, saying: "Going therefore now, teach ye all nations, baptizing them in the name of the Father, and of the Son, and of the Holy Spirit, teaching them to observe all things whatsoever I have commanded you; and behold I am with you all days even to the consummation of the world." And again He saith: "Going therefore into the whole world, preach the Gospel to every creature. And he that believeth and is baptized shall be saved; but he that believeth not shall be condemned." And again: "This Gospel of the Kingdom shall be preached in the whole world for a testimony to all nations; and then shall the end come."

And in like manner the Lord, foretelling by the prophet, saith: "And it shall come to pass in the last days, saith the Lord, I will pour out of my Spirit upon all flesh; and your sons and your daughters shall prophesy, and your young men shall see visions, and your old men shall dream dreams. And upon my servants, indeed, and upon my handmaids, will I pour out in those days of my Spirit, and they shall prophesy." And He saith in Osee: "And I will call them who were not my people, my people;...and her that had not obtained mercy, one that hath obtained mercy. And it shall be, in the place where it was said,

'Ye are not my people,' there they shall be called the sons of the living God."

41. How, then, are the people of Ireland, who never had the knowledge of God, but until now worshipped idols and unclean things, how are they lately been made a people of the Lord, and are called the sons of God? The sons of the Scots and the daughters of their kings are seen to become monks and virgins of Christ.

42. And especially there was one blessed lady of Scotic birth, of noble rank, most beautiful, of full age, whom I had baptized; and after a few days she came to us for a special counsel. She told us in confidence that she had received a message from God, and it admonished her to become a virgin of Christ and so come nearer to God. Thanks be to God, on the sixth day afterwards, most admirably and most eagerly she embraced that which all virgins of Christ do. Not that they have their fathers' agreement; nay rather they endure persecution and lying reproaches from their parents. Nevertheless their number increases more and more. And we know not the number of our race who are thus regenerated, in addition to the widows and the continent.

But the women who are held in slavery suffer most keenly. Constantly they have to endure even unto terrors and threats. But the Lord gave grace to many of my handmaidens, for, although hey are forbidden still they follow courageously he example (of the others).

43. Wherefore, then, even if I wished to leave them and proceed to Britain—and glad and very ready was I to do so, going to my fatherland and my parents, and not only that, but to go as far as Gaul in order to visit the brethren, and to behold the face of the saints of my Lord—God knows how greatly I desired it! Yet I am bound by the Spirit, who witnesseth to me that if I should do this He would account me as guilty; and I fear to lose the labor which I have begun—yet not I, but Christ the Lord, who commanded me to come and to remain with them for the rest of my life, if the Lord wishes, and if He preserves me from every evil way, so that I may not sin before Him.

44. Now I hope that I ought to do this, but I do not trust myself as long as I am in this body of death, because he is strong who daily strives to turn me from the faith and from that purity of sincere religion which I have proposed to keep for Christ my Lord to the end of my life. But the flesh, our enemy, is always dragging us unto death, that is, to the allurements which end in evil. And I know in part wherein I have not led a perfect life, as other Christians have. But I confess to my Lord, and I do not blush in His presence—for I lie not, that from the time I came to know Him, in my youth, the love of God and the fear of Him grew in me, and unto this hour through God's favor, I have kept the faith.

45. Let who will laugh and mock, I shall not be silent nor conceal the signs and wonders which were shown to me by the Lord many years before they came to pass, since He knoweth all things even before the world's beginnings.

46. Therefore I ought without ceasing to give thanks to God, who oftentimes pardoned my folly and my negligence, and who, moreover, and not in one place only, might have been greatly angered with me who was chosen to be His assistant—especially when I did not quickly assent to what was shown to me, and to what the Spirit suggested. And the Lord showed mercy to me thousands and thousands of times because He saw that I was ready, but that I did not know what in my state I should do, for many were opposing this embassy of mine. Moreover they were talking among themselves behind my back, and they kept saying: "Why does this fellow thrust himself into danger amongst enemies who have no knowledge of God?" They did not say this out of malice; but it (my mission) did not seem wise in their eyes because of my rusticity, which I myself must admit. And I did not quickly recognize the grace that then was in me. Now I have that wisdom which I ought to have had before.

47. Now, therefore, with simplicity I have disclosed to you my brethren and fellow-servants, who have believed in me because of what I told you before, and now foretell you to strengthen and confirm your faith. Would that you, too, would imitate greater things and do better things! That will be my glory, for a wise son is the glory of his father.

48. You know, and God does too, in what manner I have lived from my youth amongst you in the faith of truth and in sincerity of heart. Even towards those heathens amongst whom I dwell, I have kept faith with them, and will keep it. God knoweth, I have defrauded none of them, nor do I think of doing it, for the sake of God and His Church, lest I should raise persecution against them and against all of us, and lest through me the name of God should be blasphemed; for it is written: "Woe to the man through whom the name of God is blasphemed."

49. But though I be rude in all things, nevertheless I have endeavored in some sort to keep watch over myself, even as regards the Christian brethren, and the virgins of Christ, and the devout women who of their own accord used to present me with their little gifts, and would lay some of their ornaments upon the altar; and I returned them again to them. And they were offended because I did so. But I did it on account of my hope of immortality—that I might keep myself cautiously in all things, so that the heathens might not under any pretext seize upon me or the ministry of my service, and that I should not, even in the smallest matter, give occasion to the unbelievers to defame or disparage.

50. Perchance, then, when I baptized so many thousands of men, did I hope to get from any of them even half a scruple?[1] Tell me, and I shall restore it to you. Or when the Lord ordained clergy everywhere through my mediocrity and I gave my ministrations to them for nothing if I asked from any of them so much as the price of my shoe; tell it against me, and I shall restore you more.

51. I spent money for you that they might receive me. And both amongst you and wherever I journeyed for your sake, through many perils, even in remote parts where no man dwelt, and where never had anyone come to baptize, or to ordain clergy, or to confirm the people, I have, by the bounty of the Lord, done everything, carefully and most gladly, for your salvation.

52. Sometimes I used to give presents to the kings, besides the hire that I gave to their sons, who accompany me. Nevertheless they seized me with my companions. And on that day they most eagerly desired to kill me; but my time had not yet come. And everything they found with us

[1] A half a scruple in value is about a shilling.

they plundered, and myself they bound in iron chains. And on the fourteenth day the Lord freed me from their power; and whatever was ours was restored to us for God's sake, and for the sake of the good friends whom we had provided beforehand.

53. You know also how much I spent on those who ruled in all the districts to which I used to come more frequently. For I think that I distributed among them no less than the price of fifteen men, so that you might enjoy me, and that I might always enjoy you in God. I am not sorry for it, nor is it enough for me. Still I spend and will spend more. The Lord is powerful to grant me afterwards that I myself shall be spent for your souls.

54. Behold I call God to witness upon my soul that I lie not. Nor would I write to you that there may be an occasion of flattering words or gain, not that I hope for honor from any of you. Sufficient is the honor which is not seen, but is believed on in the heart. Faithful is He that promised; He never lieth.

55. But I see that already in this present world I am exalted above measure by the Lord. And I was not worthy nor such that He should grant this to me; since I know most certainly that poverty and affliction become me better than riches and pleasures. Nay, Christ the Lord, too, was poor for our sakes. But I, wretched and

unfortunate, even should I wish for wealth, I have it not. Nor do I judge myself, for daily I expect either murder, or robbery, or enslavement, or the occurrence of some such calamity. But none of these things do I fear, on account of the promises of heaven! I have cast myself into the hands of God Almighty, for He rules everywhere, as the prophet saith: "Cast thy care upon God, and He shall sustain thee."

56. Behold, now, I commend my soul to my most faithful God, for whom I am an ambassador in my ignoble condition; only because He accepteth no person and chose me for this office that I should be one of His ministers, but amongst His least.

57. And now what shall I render to the Lord for all the things He hath rendered to me? Nay what shall I say, or what shall I promise to my Lord? For I see nothing except that He Himself hath given to me. But He who searcheth the hearts and reins knoweth that fully and greatly do I desire, and have long been ready, that He should grant to me to drink of His chalice, as He hath granted to others also who love Him.

58. Wherefore may it never happen to me from my God that I should ever lose His people whom He purchased at the ends of the earth. I pray God to grant me perseverance, and to deign that I render myself a faithful witness to Him until my passing hence for the sake of my God.

59. And if ever I accomplished anything good for the sake of my God whom I love, I beg Him to grant me that I may shed my blood with those exiles and captives for His name, even though I should lack burial itself, or my corpse most miserably be torn limb from limb by dogs and wild beasts, or the fowls of the air devour it. Most surely I am convinced that if this should happen to me I have gained my soul with my body, because without any doubt on that day we shall arise in the brightness of the sun, that is, in the glory of Christ Jesus our Redeemer, as sons of the living God and joint-heirs with Christ, and conformed to His future image; for of Him, and through Him, and in Him are all things: to Him be glory for ever and ever. Amen. For in Him truly we shall reign.

60. For that sun which we see is raised daily for us by God's command; but it will never reign, not will its splendor endure; but all those who worship it shall go in misery to sore punishment. Not so we, who believe in and worship the true sun, Christ, who will never perish nor will anyone who doeth His will; but he will abide forever, just as Christ will abide forever, who reigneth with God the Father Almighty and with the Holy Spirit before the ages, and now, and for ever and ever. Amen.

61. Lo, again and again, I shall briefly set forth the words of my confession. I testify in truth and in the joy of my heart before God and His holy angels that I never had any motive except the Gospel and its promises for ever returning to that nation from whence previously I had barely made my escape.

62. But I pray those who believe and fear God, whosoever shall have deigned to look upon or receive this writing which Patrick, a sinner, and unlearned as everybody knows, composed in Ireland, that no one ever say it was my ignorance that did whatever small matter I did, or proved in accordance with God's good pleasure. But judge ye, and let it be most truly believed that it was the gift of God. And this is my confession before I die.

Letter to the Soldiers of Coroticus

1. I, Patrick the sinner, unlearned as everybody knows, avow that I have been established a bishop in Ireland. Most assuredly I believe that I have received from God what I am. And so I dwell in the midst of barbarous heathens, a stranger and an exile for the love of God. He is witness that this is so. Not that I desired to utter from my mouth anything so harshly and so roughly; but I am compelled, roused as I am by zeal for God and for the truth of Christ; and by love for my nearest friends and sons, for whom I have given up my fatherland and parents, yea, and my life to the point of death. I have vowed to my God to teach the heathens if I am worthy, though I be despised by some.

2. With my own hand I have written and composed these words to be given and delivered and sent to the soldiers of Coroticus; I do not say to my fellow-citizens, or to the fellow-citizens of the holy Romans, but to those who are the fellow-citizens of the demons, because of their evil works. Behaving like enemies, they are dead while they live, allies of the Scots and the apostate Picts, as though wishing to gorge themselves with the blood of innocent Christians, whom I, in countless numbers, have begotten to God, and confirmed in Christ.

3. On the day following that on which the newly-baptized, vested in white garments, were anointed with chrism—it was still fragrant on their foreheads while they were cruelly butchered and slaughtered with the sword by the above-mentioned marauders—I sent a letter with a holy priest, whom I taught from his infancy, accompanied by other clerics, to request that they would allow us some of the booty, or of the baptized captives whom they had taken. They jeered at them.

4. Therefore I know not what I should rather mourn, whether those who are slain, or those whom they captured, or those whom the devil grievously ensnared. In everlasting punishment they will become slaves of hell along with him, for verily whosoever committeth sin is a slave, and is called a son of the Devil.

5. Wherefore let every man that feareth God know that aliens they are from me and from Christ my God, for whom I am an ambassador. They are parricides, fratricides, ravening wolves that eat the people of the Lord as they eat bread. As he (the psalmist) saith: "O Lord, the ungodly have destroyed Thy law," which in more recent times He had excellently and kindly planted in Ireland, and which was built up by the favor of God.

6. I make no false claim. I have part with those whom He called and predestined to preach the Gospel amidst no small persecutions even unto the very ends of the earth, even though the enemy manifests his envy for me by means of the tyranny of Coroticus, who fears neither God nor His priests whom He chose, and to whom He granted that highest, divine and sublime power, that whom they should bind on earth should be bound in heaven.

7. Whence therefore, I beseech you earnestly, ye men, holy and humble of heart, it is not right to pay court to such men, nor to take food and drink with them, nor ought one accept their alms-givings, until by doing hard penance, with shedding of tears, they make amends before God, and liberate the servants of God and the baptized handmaidens of Christ, for whom He died and was crucified.

8. "The Most High approveth not the gifts of the wicked.... He that offereth sacrifice of the goods of the poor is as one that sacrificeth the son in the presence of his father." "The riches," he saith, "which he had gathered unjustly will be vomited up from his belly. The angel of death draggeth him away. He will be tormented by the fury of dragons. The viper's tongue shall slay him; unquenchable fire devoureth him." And therefore, "Woe to those who fill themselves with what is not their own." Or again, "What doth it profit a man if he gain the whole world, and suffer the loss of his own soul?"

9. It would be tedious to discuss or declare (their deeds) one by one, to gather from the whole law testimonies concerning such greed. Avarice is a deadly sin. "Thou shalt not covet thy neighbor's goods. Thou shalt not kill." A murderer cannot be with Christ. "He that hateth his brother" is reckoned as "a murderer." Or, again, "He that loveth not his brother abideth in death." How much more guilty is he that hath stained his hands with the blood of the sons of God, whom He recently gained in the ends of the earth through the exhortations of my littleness.

10. Did I come to Ireland without God, or according to the flesh? Who compelled me—I am bound by the Spirit—not to see anyone of my kinsfolk? Is it from me that I show godly compassion towards that nation who once took me captive and harried the menservants and the maidservants of my father's house? I was freeborn according to the flesh. I am born of a father who was a decurion. But I sold my nobility, I blush not to state it, nor am I sorry, for the profit of others. In short I am a slave in Christ to a foreign nation on account of the unspeakable glory of the eternal life which is in Christ Jesus our Lord.

11. And if my own know me not, a prophet hath no honor in his own country. Perchance we are not of one and the same fold, nor have one God and Father. As He saith: "He that is not with Me is against Me, and he that gathereth not with Me, scattereth." It is not meet that one pulleth down and another buildeth up. I seek not the things which are my own.

It was not my own grace, but God who put this earnest care into my heart, that I should be one of the hunters and fishers whom long ago God foretold would come in the last days.

12. Men look askance at me. What shall I do, O Lord? I am exceedingly despised. Lo, around me are thy sheep torn to pieces and spoiled, and by the robbers aforesaid, on the orders of Coroticus with hostile intent. Far from the love of God is he who betrays Christians into the hands of the Scots and the Picts. Raving wolves have swallowed up the flock of the Lord, which verily in Ireland was growing up excellently with the greatest care. And the sons of Scots and the daughters of chieftains who were monks and virgins of Christ, I am unable to reckon. Wherefore, "Be not pleased with the wrong done to the just; even unto hell it shall not please."

13. Which of the saints would not shudder to jest or to enjoy a feast with such men? They have filled their houses with the spoil of dead Christians. They live by plunder. Wretched men, they know not that it is deadly poison which they offer as food to their friends and sons; just as Eve did not understand that verily it was death that she handed to her husband. So are all they who do wrong. They work death eternal as their punishment.

14. The custom of the Roman Christian Gauls is this: they send holy and able men to the Franks and other heathens with many thousands of *solidi* to redeem baptized captives. But thou, so often, slayest them, or sellest them to a foreign nation that knows not God. Thou deliverest the members of Christ as it were into a brothel. What manner of hope in God has thou, or whosoever consents with thee, or who converses with thee in words of flattery? God will judge; for it is written: "Not only those who do evil, but those who consent with them, shall be damned."

15. I know not what I should say, or what I should speak further about the departed ones of the sons of God, whom the sword has touched sharply above measure. For it is written: "Weep with them that weep," and again, "If one member suffer, let all the members suffer with it." The Church, therefore, bewails and will lament her sons and daughters whom the sword has not yet slain, but who were enslaved and carried off to distant lands, where sin abounds openly, grossly and shamelessly. There freemen are put up for sale, Christians are made slaves, and, worst of all, slaves of the most shameful, most vile and apostate Picts.

16. Therefore, in sadness and grief shall I cry aloud: O most fair and most beloved brethren and sons whom I begot in Christ—the number I cannot reckon—what shall I do for you? I am not worthy to come to the aid either of God or men. The wickedness of the wicked hath prevailed over us. We have been made, as it were, strangers. Perchance they do not believe that we received one baptism (with them), or that we have the same God and Father. It is in their eyes a shameful thing that we were born in Ireland. As the prophet saith: "Have ye not one God? Why have ye, every one of you, forsaken his neighbor?"

17. Therefore I grieve for you, I grieve, O ye most dear to me. But again, I rejoice within myself. I have not labored for nothing, and my journeying to a strange land was not in vain. And yet, there has happened a crime so horrible and unspeakable! Thank God, it was as baptized believers that ye departed from the world to Paradise. I can see you. Ye have begun to remove to where there shall be no night, nor sorrow, nor death any more; but ye shall leap like calves loosened from their bonds, and ye shall tread down the wicked, and they shall be ashes under your feet.

18. Ye therefore shall reign with apostles, and prophets, and martyrs. Ye shall take possession of everlasting kingdoms, as He Himself witnesseth, saying: "They shall come from the east and the west, and shall sit down with Abraham and Isaac and Jacob in the kingdom of heaven." "Without are dogs and sorcerers and murderers; and liars and false swearers shall have their portion in the lake of everlasting fire" (Apoc. 22:15; 21:8). Doth not the apostle rightly say: "Where the just man shall scarcely be saved, where shall the sinner and the ungodly transgressor of the law find himself?"

19. Well then, where shall Coroticus with his iniquitous followers, rebels against Christ, where will they see themselves, they who distribute baptized young women as booty—and that for a miserable temporal kingdom, which truly passes away in a moment like a cloud or like smoke which is verily dispersed by the wind? So shall the deceitful wicked perish at the presence of the Lord; but the just shall feast in great constancy with Christ. They shall judge nations, and shall have dominion over wicked kings for ever and ever. Amen.

20. I testify before God and His angels that it will be so as He has signified to my unskillfulness. The words are not mine which I have set forth in Latin, but they are God's and the apostles' and the prophets', who have never lied. "He that believeth shall be saved, but he that believeth not shall be condemned." For "God hath spoken."

21. I beseech earnestly that whichever servant of God be ready that he be the bearer of this letter, so that on no account it be suppressed by anyone, but much rather be read in the presence of all the people, yea, in the presence of Coroticus himself. If it so be, may God inspire them sometime to amend their lives for God, so that even though late they may repent their impious deeds (murderers of the brethren of the Lord), and may liberate the baptized women captives whom they had taken, so that they may deserve to live to God, and be made whole, here and in eternity.

Peace to the Father, and to the Son, and to the Holy Spirit. Amen.

PHOTO BY THE AUTHOR

St. Patrick's
Catholic Cathedral
Armagh.
Begun, 1840
Halted by the Famine, 18
Work resumed, 1854
Completed, 1873
Consecrated, 1904

PHOTO BY THE AUTH

St. Patrick's Protestant Cathedral.
Armagh.

Probably somewhere in the vicinity of the square Tower of the restored cathedral was the location of St. Patrick's first church, the mother-church of Irish Catholicism.

APPENDICES

APPENDIX ONE
Textual References for the Virtues of St. Patrick

(These are the virtues found in the *Confession* and the *Letter to the Soldiers of Coroticus.* The numerals indicate the paragraphs of the documents. C - indicates the *Confession,* L - indicates the *Letter.)*

CHARITY
- C 13, 23, 26
- L 3, 7, 10, 12, 14, 15, 16, 17, 21

CONFIDENCE AND TRUST IN GOD
- C 11, 13, 14, 17, 19, 20, 24, 25, 26, 29, 30, 32, 33, 34, 40, 45, 54, 55, 60
- L 1, 10, 20

APPENDIX TWO

The Hymn of St. Secundinus

A Hymn in Praise of St. Patrick

The "Hymn of St. Secundinus"[1] is presented in this appendix because it is a contemporary's description of St. Patrick laboring at his apostolate. It is intimate, and it is extensive; and hence it affords a deeper understanding of the legacy which St. Patrick prepared for his people and their posterity.

Ancient Irish tradition unanimously attributes the hymn to Secundinus, and to him alone; modern scholars generally accept his authorship. There is the strongest internal evidence that the work was composed during the lifetime of St. Patrick. St. Secundinus died in 447, a decade and a half before St. Patrick's demise. There is a great possibility, as Père Grosjean suggested, that the hymn might have been written in the interval between the *Letter to the Soldiers of Coroticus* and the *Confession.*[2] In that case it would be a defense of Patrick against his critics by an eyewitness, his most trusted assistant bishop. The listing of Patrick's employments, contained in the hymn, contributed valuable additions to the meager and vague descriptions of the *Confession.* This fact alone makes the hymn most important.

St. Secundinus was one of the three bishops who in 439 came from Gaul to assist St. Patrick. The Irish called him Sechnall, and his poem, "The Hymn of St. Sechnall." St. Patrick reposed great confidence in him, locating the

---

[1]The author wishes gratefully to acknowledge the permission of the Society for the Promotion of Christian Knowledge, of London, to use "The Hymn of St. Sechnall," 'Hymnus in Laudem Sancti Patricii,' which appears in their publication, *The Writings of St. Patrick*, translated by Newport J. D. White, D.D.; London, 1932.

[2]Père Grosjean, with Professor Bieler, hold as most likely that the *Letter* was written before the *Confession.*

site of Sechnall's church at a place only four miles from Tara, where was the dwelling of the High-King of Ireland. The name of the devoted coadjutor was always ranked second to Patrick's own; thus the heading of the earliest collection of canons for the ruling of the Irish Church reads: "Patrick, Secundinus, Auxilius, and Iserninus."[1]

The Hymn of St. Secundinus comprises twenty-three stanzas, each consisting of four long lines. It is an alphabetical hymn, which means that the initial letters of the first word in each stanza are used in the order of the alphabet. In the English translation, here printed, each stanza is headed by the first Latin word. In comparing the initial letters of these Latin words, the alphabetical order can be perceived. St. Secundinus' poem is the earliest of the numerous Latin hymns which were written in Ireland. But always the primary importance of the "Hymn of St. Secundinus" lies in this: it is a faithful, loyal account, by an eyewitness, of his leader's holy virtues and zealous deeds. After all, these are the essential elements of the legacy of St. Patrick.

I. *AUDITE.*

Hear, all ye who love God, the holy merits
of Patrick the bishop, a man blessed in Christ;
how, for his good deeds, he is likened unto the angels
and, for his perfect life, is comparable to the apostles.

II. *BEATA.*

In all things he keepeth Christ's blessed commandments;
his works shine forth brightly among men:
and these follow his holy, wonderful example;
whence, also, they magnify the Lord, the Father in heaven.

III. *CONSTANS.*

Steadfast in the fear of God, and in faith immovable,
upon him, as upon Peter, the Church is built;

[1] *Saint Patrick*, Eoin MacNeill, New York, 1934, p. 74.

and he hath been allotted his apostleship by God;
against him the gates of hell prevail not.

IV. *DOMINUS.*

The Lord chose him to teach the barbarous nations,
and to fish with the nets of doctrine:
and from the world to draw believers unto grace,
who should follow the Lord to the ethereal abode.

V. *ELECTA.*

He tradeth with Christ's choice Gospel-talents,
which among the Irish tribes he doth require with interest:
hereafter, as reward for the pains of this labor or voyaging,
he shall possess the joy of the heavenly kingdom with
Christ.

VI. *FIDELIS.*

The faithful servant and eminent messenger of God,
he showeth good men an apostolic example and pattern:
to God's folk he preacheth by acts as well as by words,
that he
may stir up by good deeds the man whom he converteth
not by speech.

VII. *GLORIAM.*

With Christ he hath glory, in the world honor;
he is venerated by all as an angel of God;
him hath God sent, like Paul, as an apostle to the Gentiles,
that he might lead the way for men unto the Kingdom
of God.

VIII. *HUMILIS.*

Humble in spirit and body through the fear of God,
upon him, for his good deeds, the Lord resteth;
in his righteous flesh he beareth the *stigmata* of Christ;
and in his cross alone doth glory, staying himself thereon.

IX. *IMPIGER.*

Unwearied, he feedeth believers with celestial repasts,
lest those who are seen in Christ's company should faint by the way:
to these he distributeth, as loaves, Gospel-words:
and in his hands they are multiplied, as was the manna.

X. *KASTAM.*

For the love of the Lord he keepeth chaste his flesh;
which flesh he hath prepared as a temple for the Holy Spirit:
by whom, in pure activities, it is continually possessed;
and he doth offer it to God as a living and acceptable sacrifice.

XI. *LUMENQUE.*

And he is the great, burning Gospel-light of the world *(mundi);*
raised upon a candlestick, shining through the whole world *(saeculo):*
the King's fortified city, set upon a hill;
wherein is much store which the Lord doth possess.

XII. *MAXIMUS.*

For the greatest in the kingdom of heaven shall he be called
who fulfilleth in good actions what by sacred words he teacheth:
he excelleth as a good example and pattern to the faithful:
and in a pure heart he hath confidence toward God.

XIII. *NOMEN.*

He proclaimeth boldly to the tribes the Name of the Lord,
to whom he giveth the eternal grace of the laver of salvation:
for their offenses he prayeth daily unto God;
for them also he offers up to God worthy sacrifices *(dignas immolat hostias).*

XIV. *OMNEM.*

All the glory of the world he spurneth for the law divine;
all things, compared with His (God's) table he counteth as chaff:
nor is he moved by the violent thunderbolt of this world,
but rejoiceth in afflictions when he doth suffer for Christ.

XV. *PASTOR.*

The good and faithful shepherd of the Gospel-flock,
him hath God chosen to guard the people of God:
to feed with divine doctrine his own folk, for whose sake,
after Christ's example, he disregardeth his life.

XVI. *QUEM.*

Him, for his merits, hath the Savior advanced to be pontiff,
to exhort the clergy in their heavenly warfare:
to them he distributeth heavenly food with clothing,
and this is supplied in his divine and sacred discourses.

XVII. *REGIS.*

As the King's messenger bidding believers to the marriage,
he is adorned, clad in a wedding garment:
in heavenly vessels he draweth out heavenly wine;
offering drink to God's folk in a spiritual cup.

XVIII. *SACRUM.*

In the Sacred Volume sacred treasure he findeth;
and in the Savior's flesh discerneth Deity:
this treasure he buyeth with his holy and perfect methods;
Israel is his soul's name, as "seeing God."

XIX. *TESTIS.*

The Lord's faithful witness in the Catholic law,
his words are seasoned with the divine oracles:
lest human flesh decay, and of worms be eaten;
but with heavenly savor be salted as a sacrifice *(ad victimam).*

XX. *VERUS.*

The true and eminent tiller of the Gospel-field,
his deeds are seen to be the Gospels of Christ;
these, with divine mouth, he soweth in the ears of the prudent,
whose hearts and minds he ploweth up with the Holy Spirit.

XXI. *XTUS.*

Christ hath chosen him for himself to be his vicar on earth;
from two-fold slavery he doth set captives free:
very many he hath redeemed from slavery to men;
countless numbers he releaseth from the Devil's thrall.

XXII. *YMNOS.*

Hymns, with the Apocalypse and the Psalms of God, he singeth,
and doth expound the same for the edifying of God's people:
this law he holdeth in the Trinity of the Sacred Name,
and teacheth One Substance in Three Persons.

XXIII. *ZONA.*

Girded with the Lord's girdle, day and night,
without intermission he prayeth unto God, the Lord:
hereafter to receive the reward of his mighty labor,
as a saint, he shall reign with the Apostles over Israel.

APPENDIX THREE

The Lorica, or Breastplate, of St. Patrick

The *Lorica*[1] is an ancient Gaelic prayer which has been attributed to St. Patrick. It is an invocation of the Holy Trinity, and was usually recited in the morning. In the early Irish Church loricas were numerous; some were written in Gaelic and some in Latin. *Lorica,* a Latin word, originally signified a piece of protective armor, a breastplate. This particular lorica has often been called the *Breastplate of St. Patrick.* Lorica-prayers were recited to obtain divine protection against evils, physical or spiritual, especially against the powers of darkness. The loricas replaced heathen incantations, when the Irish embraced Christianity.

The *Lorica* of St. Patrick in its present form was written down most probably in the ninth century. Experts in the Gaelic language, however, feel that its syntax, metrical forms, and sentiments argue to a far older composition, possibly of the sixth century, or even earlier. In the Ireland of those days an oral composition could have been made, which might not have been committed to the written page until some centuries later.

---

[1] *The Irish Liber Hymnorum,* J. H. Bernard, D.D., and R. Atkinson, LL.D., Vols. I and II, London, 1898. Henry Bradshaw Society.

Dr. Bieler, while admitting that St. Patrick's authorship cannot be proved, says that the possibility of St. Patrick's authorship should not be rashly disavowed. This scholar, the foremost modern Patrician authority, includes the *Lorica* in his excellent volume, *The Works of St. Patrick.*[1] And rightly, because the *Lorica* is one of the earliest implementations of the legacy of St. Patrick.

I.

I bind to myself today
    The strong power of an invocation of the Trinity,
    The faith of the Trinity in Unity,
    The Creator of the Universe.

II.

I bind to myself today
    The might of the Incarnation of Christ with that of His Baptism,
    The might of His Crucifixion with that of His Burial,
    The might of His Resurrection with that of His Ascension,
    The might of His Coming on the Judgment Day.

[1] "The Lorica," p. 76. *The Works of St. Patrick, St. Secundinus' Hymn on St. Patrick.* The Newman Press, Westminster, Maryland; Longmans, Green and Co., London, 1953.

III.

I bind to myself today
The power in the love of the Seraphim,
In the obedience of the Angels,
In the ministration of the Archangels,
In the hope of Resurrection unto reward,
In the prayers of the Patriarchs,
In the predictions of the Prophets,
In the preaching of the Apostles,
In the faith of the Confessors,
In the purity of the holy Virgins,
In the deeds of Righteous men.

IV.

I bind to myself today
The power of Heaven,
The brightness of the Sun,
The whiteness of Snow,
The splendor of Fire,
The speed of Lightning,
The swiftness of Wind,
The depth of the Sea,
The stability of the Earth,
The firmness of Rocks.

V.

I bind to myself today
God's Power to pilot me,
God's Might to uphold me,
God's Wisdom to teach me,
God's Eye to watch over me,
God's Ear to hear me,

God's Word to give me speech,
God's Hand to guide me,
God's Way to lie before me,
God's Shield to shelter me,
God's Host to secure me,
Against the snares of demons,
Against the seductions of vices,
Against the lusts of nature,
Against everyone who meditates injury to me,
Whether far or near,
Whether few or with many.

VI.

I invoke today all these virtues
Against every hostile merciless power
Which may assail my body and my soul,
Against the incantations of false prophets,
Against the black laws of heathenism,
Against the false laws of heresy,
Against the deceits of idolatry,
Against the spells of women, and smiths, and druids,
Against every knowledge that blinds the soul of man.

VII.

Christ protect me today
Against poison, against burning,
Against drowning, against wounding,
That I may receive abundant reward.

VIII.

Christ with me, Christ before me,
Christ behind me, Christ within me,
Christ under me, Christ above me,
Christ at my right, Christ at my left,
Christ in lying down, Christ in sitting, Christ
in rising up.

IX.

Christ in the heart of every man who thinks of me,
Christ in the mouth of every man who speaks to
me,
Christ in every eye that sees me,
Christ in every ear that hears me.

X.

I bind to myself today
The strong power of an invocation of the
Trinity,
The faith of the Trinity in Unity,
The Creator of the Universe.

XI.

Salvation is of the Lord,
Salvation is of the Lord,
Salvation is of Christ;
May Thy salvation, O Lord, be with us
forever.

(All verses are in Gaelic, save the last (XI) which is in Latin.)

IMPORTANT DATES

View of Saint Patrick's Life

YEAR	
387	Birth of Saint Patrick
403	Captivity in Ireland
409	Escape to Gaul, return to Britain
412	Religious journeying in Gaul
417	Monastic life in Auxerre, under Saint Germanus
432	Beginning of the Irish Mission (Consecration as bishop by Saint Germanus)
439	Assistant bishops from Gaul (Secundinus, Auxilius and Iserninus)
441	Approval of Saint Patrick by Pope Saint Leo the Great
444	Founding of Armagh, the chief bishopric
452	The time of the writing of the *Letter to the Soldiers of Coroticus* and the *Confession*
461	Death of Saint Patrick

(THE DATES MOSTLY ARE APPROXIMATE.)

PHOTO BY THE AUTHOR.

St. Patrick's Memorial
A Thousanth Year Tribute

Clonmacnoise

Clonmacnoise, most outstanding among the Irish monastic schools, chosen place of burial for numerous Gaelic kings, was also the seat of an ancient Irish diocese, stretching quietly along the east bank of the Shannon through the center of Ireland. The abbey's chief church was the cathedral of the diocese. A fifteenth-century alteration put this fine Gothic arch into its north wall. In the space above the arch were carved three figures: St. Patrick, in the center; St. Dominic on one side of him, and St. Francis on the other. A Latin inscription makes known that, "Dom. Odo, Decanus, me fecit." (Dom Odo the Deacon made me). Dom Odo was Dom Hugh O'Maol Eoin (O'Malone), Deacon of the cathedral. Of great significance is the date, 1461. That year was held by most people as the one thousandth anniversary of the death of St. Patrick. One thousand years of venerating Ireland's national apostle! One thousand years of being inspired by St. Patrick's prayers and deeds.

Daughters of St. Paul

IN MASSACHUSETTS
50 St. Paul's Avenue, Boston, Ma. 02130
172 Tremont Street, Boston, Ma. 02111
IN NEW YORK
78 Fort Place, Staten Island, N.Y. 10301
59 East 43rd Street, New York, N.Y. 10017
625 East 187th Street, Bronx, N.Y. 10458
525 Main Street, Buffalo, N.Y. 14203
IN NEW JERSEY
Hudson Mall — Route 440 and
Communipaw Avenue, Jersey City, N.J. 07304
IN CONNECTICUT
202 Fairfield Avenue, Bridgeport, Ct. 06604
IN OHIO
2105 Ontario St. (at Prospect Ave.), Cleveland,
Oh. 44115
25 E. Eighth Street, Cincinnati, Oh. 45202
IN PENNSYLVANIA
1719 Chestnut Street, Philadelphia, Pa. 19103
IN FLORIDA
2700 Biscayne Blvd., Miami, Fl. 33137
IN LOUISIANA
4403 Veterans Memorial Blvd., Metairie, La. 70002
1800 South Acadian Thruway, P.O. Box 2028,
Baton Rouge, La. 70802
IN MISSOURI
1001 Pine Street (at North 10th), St. Louis, Mo. 63101
IN TEXAS
114 East Main Plaza, San Antonio, Tx. 78205
IN CALIFORNIA
1570 Fifth Avenue, San Diego, Ca. 92101
46 Geary Street, San Francisco, Ca. 94108
IN HAWAII
1143 Bishop Street, Honolulu, Hi. 96813
IN ALASKA
750 West 5th Avenue, Anchorage, Ak. 99501
IN CANADA
3022 Dufferin Street, Toronto 395, Ontario, Canada
IN ENGLAND
57, Kensington Church Street, London W. 8, England
IN AUSTRALIA
58 Abbotsford Rd., Homebush, N.S.W., Sydney 2140,
Australia